WAR[CRY]

UNLEASHING YOUR VOICE IN A WORLD OF SILENCE

Natalie Barnoske

Copyright © 2016 by Natalie Barnoske.

All rights reserved. No part of this publication may be reproduced, distributed or transmitted in any form or by any means, including photocopying, recording, or other electronic or mechanical methods, without the prior written permission of the publisher, except in the case of brief quotations embodied in critical reviews and certain other noncommercial uses permitted by copyright law. For permission requests, contact the publisher.

Published in Houston Texas, by Battle Ground Creative
Second Edition

Battle Ground Creative is a faith-based publishing company with an emphasis on helping first-time authors find their voice. Named after an obscure city in Washington State, we currently operate offices in Houston, Texas and Princeton, New Jersey. For a complete title list and bulk order information, please visit www.battlegroundcreative.com

All Scripture quotations, unless otherwise indicated, are taken from the Holy Bible, New International Version®. NIV®. Copyright © 1973, 1978, 1984, 2011 by International Bible Society. Used by permission of Zondervan. All rights reserved.

Scripture quotations marked "CEB" are taken from the Common English Bible, copyright © 2010 by Common English Bible Committee. Published by Christian Resources Development Corporation. All rights reserved.

Scripture quotations marked "MSG" are taken from The Message®, copyright © 1993, 1994, 1995, 1996, 2000, 2001, 2002 by Eugene H. Peterson. Published by NavPress. All rights reserved.

Scripture quotations marked "ESV" are taken from the English Standard Version Bible, copyright © 2001, 2007, 2011 by Crossway Bibles, a ministry of the Good News Publishers. Published by Crossway Bibles. All rights reserved.

Scripture quotations marked "MEV" are taken from the Holy Bible, Modern English Version, copyright © 2014 by Military Bible Association. Published by Passio (Charisma House). All rights reserved.

Scripture quotations marked "AMP" are taken from the Amplified Bible, copyright © 1954, 1958, 1962, 1964, 1965, 1987, 2015. By Zondervan and The Lockman Foundation. Published by Zondervan. All rights reserved.

Scripture quotations marked "TLB" are taken from The Living Bible, copyright © 1971 by Tyndale House Publishers, Kenneth N. Taylor, Ed. Published by Tyndale House Publishers. All rights reserved.

Scripture quotations marked "NRSV" are taken from the New Revised Standard Version Bible, copyright © 1989 by the Division of Christian Education of the National Council of the Churches of Christ in the USA. Published by Thomas Nelson. All rights reserved.

Scripture quotations marked "ASV" are taken from The American Standard Version Bible, copyright © Public Domain.

Scripture quotations marked "NLV" are taken from the New Life Version Bible, copyright © 1969 by Christian Literature International. Published by Christian Literature International. All rights reserved.

Cover photograph: Depositphoto

ISBN-10: 0-9908738-6-2
ISBN-13: 978-0-9908738-6-0
RELIGION / Christian Life / Spiritual Growth

Printed in the United States of America

*To campus missionaries and young leaders everywhere.
Rise up and break through the silence.*

If you want to rise in your purpose and become a voice for your generation, Natalie Barnoske's book, WarCry, is for you. God has not called you to be an echo but a voice of Truth that will give hope to those around you. This book will strengthen the calling God has placed on your life and release the boldness you need to make a difference.

– Jim and Dawn Raley, Lead Pastors
Calvary Christian Center, Ormond Beach, Florida

Are you ready for a WarCry? Natalie does not write to entertain a generation, but to empower them! Though you will read it in silence, WarCry shouts to a generation. Natalie writes from her painful past to boldly proclaim Christ's victory, with each word being prophetically penned with the voice of the Spirit. 'Silence is no longer an option,' Natalie writes. WarCry is her war cry to teenagers, to no longer remain silent in their lives. It's time to shout!

– Rod Whitlock, Author and Speaker
www.rodwhitlock.com

WarCry is more than a book; it's a movement of students passionate about reaching their peers. Now is the time for a generation to step up and lead the way. I believe WarCry will inspire students and leaders to take their God-given place and make a difference in this dark world.

– Al Force, Lead Pastor
Oceanway Assembly of God, Jacksonville, Florida
Former District Youth Director, Pen FL Assemblies of God

In every generation, God uses specific leaders to initiate radical transformation. They challenge people to break fear and respond with intensity to the mission at hand. Natalie is boldly leading the charge and stirring up warriors to seek and save the lost. WarCry is not just a book, rather a declaration to the enemy that God's people will not be intimidated. It is calling every believer to rise up, to prepare for battle, and to fight.

– Joseph Barnoske, Evangelist and Missionary
Pen Florida Youth Alive

The ministry imprinted on the pages of this book will bring challenge and encouragement to everyone who reads its powerful message. More importantly, the truths presented will equip every leader and warrior to be their best in the battle to advance God's Kingdom in this generation. Though Satan is attempting to bully the rising generation into silence, Natalie Barnoske effectively guides them toward their rightful positions as leaders, prophets, and kings, and provides the information, tools and weapons needed to be successful in the fight for the souls of humanity and the culture of our nation. She weaves Scriptural examples with the testimonies of leaders to guide disciples in their quest to become warriors, then leaders, then champions! The Body of Christ will be more powerful and better equipped for warfare after reading this book.

Natalie has surrendered to the Holy Spirit and call of God and, along with her husband Joe, has taken a leadership role in ministry to become a true "Deborah" of our time. Her faith, courage, and commitment is etched upon these pages. As one reads, they experience that message. A strong desire forms to join the WarCry needed in this critically important spiritual generation. Sound your WarCry. Join the battle!

– Terry Raburn, Superintendent
Peninsular Florida District of the Assemblies of God
Chairman, Board of Trustees, Southeastern University

Contents

Foreword ix

Introduction xi

[1] Modern-Day Warrior 1

[2] Silence is No Longer an Option 13

[3] Cry of a Champion 23

WarCry of a Leader

[4] Wide Awake 35

[5] Arise for Battle 45

[6] No Trespassing 55

WarCry of a Prophet

[7] Elijah's Cry 67

[8] Born to Roar 77

[9] Chain-Breaker, History-Maker 87

WarCry of a King

[10] The Armor of Light 99

[11] David's Stand 109

[12] Mountain-Mover Generation 119

Unleash Your WarCry

[13] Army of Artists 133

[14] Unleashed 141

[15] Live Dangerously 149

A Challenge to the "Now" Generation	161
Notes	167
Acknowledgements	169
About the Author	171

Foreword

Silence is not an option for the true follower of Jesus. God created you with a divine plan and purpose. He's given you a story to tell and a message to share. His plan is for you to use your story for His glory by sharing the message of His incredible love, and He's given you a unique voice with which to share it.

Discovering God's plan for my voice has been an amazing journey. As a shy, quiet, 14-year-old who didn't want to attend youth camp, I had no idea what God had in store for my life. After riding in the back of the bus, disconnected from those around me—and certainly from God—I stepped off the bus and into a weekend that would forever change my life. God filled me with His Holy Spirit and gave me boldness to overcome my shy personality as I shared the truth to my friends at school, on my football team, and in my neighborhood. I certainly didn't always share it perfectly, but by God's grace, I continue to share it passionately.

Unfortunately, many who claim to follow Christ have allowed the intimidation of our culture to reduce their WarCry to a whisper—and the Church wonders why we are making so little headway in our mission.

Natalie Barnoske is like a stick of spiritual dynamite. She's been chosen by God to not only lift her own voice but to awaken others to do the same. She and her husband, Joe, have given their lives to reaching and mobilizing a generation for God's Kingdom work. As you read this book, you will sense her passion and wisdom, and be inspired by her personal stories of how God is at work in these last days.

Just like the biblical examples and modern day world changers in each chapter, you too are called to be a warrior. Now is the time. Lift your voice. The world is waiting.

Scotty Gibbons
Author and Speaker
www.scottygibbons.com

Introduction

I am a missionary-evangelist who believes deeply in the unique calling on this generation of young leaders.

This means that I believe in you.

There is potential and power inside of you that has yet to be released.

You were born to be dangerous to the kingdom of darkness.

Together, we are a chosen generation and a royal priesthood. We are an army of God's people with an unprecedented calling for this time period. For this reason, I am confident that this is a word for you.

When you first hear the words "war cry," you may envision Mel Gibson taking his final stance as Scottish rebel leader William Wallace, or an ancient warrior preparing his soldiers for battle. At least, I did. Until the Lord showed me that modern times call for a reinterpretation of what it means to release a WarCry.

A WarCry is not just a phrase from the ancient days of battle. It is your unique expression of God's creative power and victorious love. It awakens the armies of the Lord and scares off the enemy. Without it, you are helpless in warfare. With it, there is nothing you cannot do. It shakes off all fear and positions you to do great exploits for the Kingdom of God. **Take it from me: Jesus did not save you to make you silent.**

This book will expose the attack of silence and respond with biblical, historical, and modern war cries from different people who were unlikely to be called warriors, but we're undeniably positioned to unleash their God-given voice. This will position you to awaken your WarCry and break through the silence.

WarCry is more than a book; it is a rallying shout, a wake-up call birthed from within my spirit and evolved from my own journey. Through the guidance of the Holy Spirit, I pray that you will begin to discover the power in your unique voice and gain clarity about your divine mission.

Make no mistake about it: your personal expression of God's love is a sleeping giant, ready to be unleashed into this disillusioned world. But how you respond to the attack of silence will determine your destiny. This is important for every believer, because we are on the brink of a global breakthrough and, more than ever, our broken world needs you to awaken to God's presence, rise up, and respond with a WarCry. I'm believing that the Lord will bless you on this journey!

~Natalie.

[1]

Modern-Day Warrior

Let the weak say, "I am a warrior."
~ Joel 3:10b, ESV

EVERY WARRIOR HAS A legend: a valiant story, intertwined with overwhelming obstacles and devastating pain. Some may find their story is still a legend in the making, while others wait patiently for the first act to begin.

The question is not how does your legend begin, but rather, how will your journey unfold? Will you discover your voice and rise up to change your world, or will you fall victim to the silence of a generation?

The choice is up to you.

My legend began twelve years ago on one of those nights that you just never forget.

I hesitantly stepped through the two massive doors and entered the huge gymnasium. Filled with loud music, bright lights, and passionate people who raised their hands during worship, I just knew that this was what I had been searching for my entire life.

You have to understand that, growing up, I had no idea what it meant to be an on-fire, sold-out, passionate Christian. My dad lived as though Jesus Christ died on an old rugged cross for him to live with an old tired religion. It would take him years to realize that Jesus died for a passionate relationship.

Another reason was my mom. Mom was not a bad person but struggled every day of her life with a drug addiction. She slept all day and spent the majority of my pre-teen years in jail, or at a help house designed for recovering addicts. So, you can understand why my world flipped upside down when I gave my life to Jesus at sixteen.

That is why I could barely stand under the overwhelming presence of God that first night at X-Stream Youth Church. It was like nothing I had ever experienced before. The Holy Spirit was so tangible; I felt like I could reach out and touch Him, even though I had no idea who He even was. The entire service, I sat at the edge of my seat in an effort to grasp every word of the message. Then, the moment for the altar call came, and I just couldn't fight it off: I knew that I had to commit my life to the Lord.

That was the moment it all started.

A few weeks after surrendering my heart to Jesus, I was hit hard by a night I wish I could forget. Beneath the warm glow of our family room lights, Dad received a phone call that interrupted our quiet night. Upon returning to the room, he looked as though an urgent message needed to be transmitted immediately, but hesitation marked each step. His words were stern and solemn. "Your mom has been sick now for a long time. In fact, she has been in and out of the hospital for almost a year. Early this morning, she passed away..." His words trailed off into a sea of shock as my sister and I fought for words.

The next part was the greatest shock of all.

My dad continued to explain that her unexpected death resulted from a spider bite. A tiny, insignificant spider literally stole my mother's life. He explained that, over the course of the past year, her leg had slowly grown more infected by the poison of a brown recluse spider. The weekly hospital visits and treatments were no match for the poison, especially since her immune system was completely destroyed from a lifestyle of addiction. It's ironic how something so small and inconsequential can have such a catastrophic effect on someone's life.

I sat there in silence, waiting for my mind to catch up with the news I had just received.

It was as if my mother wore a mask. When she was using the drugs, her mask was on and everything appeared normal. Outsiders would never have guessed the struggle that our family was experiencing. Then, the mask flew off and the truth would be revealed: without illegal painkillers, she was unrecognizable.

So, she made every effort to put the mask back on and act like we had the perfect little family. Yet on the inside, she was dying.

And truthfully, so was I.

Now, everything changed. It felt as though my entire childhood was on a movie reel. Good memories flooded back, as well as the bad. To be honest, I was unsure which was worse. Was I sad, or was I angry? The horrific fights, which mainly consisted of her throwing household items at my face, were no longer a source of anger. Catching her shooting up drugs in the laundry room seemed like a distant black and white movie from decades ago. Deep emotions from the day she walked out sat in the pit of my stomach, but none of that mattered now because I didn't even get to say good-bye. In fact, until that fateful call, I didn't even know that she was sick.

All night long, as I desperately fought to sleep, the only thing I could remember was an innocent image of her face that I held in my childhood memories before she had turned into someone I didn't even recognize.

Only a few weeks after that eventful October night, my family received some startling news from the doctor's office regarding my dad's health. Over the years, my dad had slowly been showing symptoms of extreme shakiness, usually related to severe anxiety. We thought it was just stress, related to the issues with my mom. The doctor, however, had a different opinion, and he called it Parkinson's disease. He proceeded to tell my dad that, over the years, shakiness would take over and he would lose all normal body movement in his arms and legs. Although his mind would be unaffected, his body would slowly stop working, and one day he would be confined to a bed. In this moment, I accepted the charge to be my dad's primary caregiver.

Being only a few weeks old in the faith, this news was my breaking point. I remember thinking, *normal teenagers do not lose their mother to a spider bite, especially before her forties. Normal teenagers do not come to find out that their father has a degenerative disease!* I screamed on the inside, "What is going on? I just surrendered to Jesus and it seems like my world is falling apart!"

At this very moment, I was faced with a choice.

Would I quit, or choose to rise up? Would I run from God,

or stand on His truth?

Just as I had a choice to rise up, so do you.

Be encouraged; God will always make a way.

THE WAY MAKER

At the heart of every faith journey is the fact that God will always make a way. For some mysterious reason, even as a new believer, something inside of my heart pushed me toward church rather than away from it. I became convinced that God had led me into a relationship with Him at the perfect time. Looking back, I know that I would never have made it through that difficult sophomore year without the Lord by my side. Like many of you, I had every reason to run from God, but when God says there will be a way, expect Him to always come through.

Do not be discouraged; our God is a Way Maker! No matter what your situation may be, God has a way for you to reach your destiny. The Lord proclaims in Isaiah 43:19, *"Behold, I am doing a new thing; now it springs forth, do you not perceive it? I will make a way in the wilderness and rivers in the desert"* (ESV).

All throughout the Bible, God was an expert at creating a pathway when, according to human sight, none existed. Noah boldly walked the unseen path when he built the ark, despite criticism. Abraham bravely followed the unseen path as he trudged up Mt. Moriah with Isaac, intent on obeying the Lord at all costs. When Jesus called the disciples out upon the water, Peter bravely stepped out into the unseen. Moses arrived at the edge of the Red Sea with the enemy at his heels. Looking out upon the great expanse of water, his own sight revealed no pathway, but he raised his staff in faith and, out of nothing, God made a way. For the salvation of humanity, God even sent

Jesus Christ as The Way. Our omnipresent, omniscient, and omnipotent God will always make a way for His people. There is no giant too big, no valley is too deep, no water too vast, no sickness too strong, no child too far, and no past too dirty. There will always be a way!

God actually called me into ministry at age fourteen, two years prior to my first night at X-stream Youth Church. There were no fireworks or prophetic announcements. One afternoon, I was passing the local Catholic church and I heard the Holy Spirit say, "This is what you are going to do for the rest of your life."

In response, I thought, "Sorry, God! I refuse to be a nun!" Little did I know that God had a future for me in the ministry that remained true, even in the midst of these dark moments.

The pathway may have been unseen, but it was there nonetheless. Do not believe the lie that your background, mistakes, age, parents, weaknesses, or lack of education are bigger than God. Our Champion fights on our behalf, and He wants us to be free from the past, the fears, and the chains that silence us, so that we can unleash a powerful WarCry that will awaken the armies of God and strike fear into the enemy. A WarCry is harnessing the power of your words to advance the Kingdom of Heaven.

There is a WarCry stirring deep within you. Maybe your story has silenced it, but God is ready to resurrect it!

War Cry: A Warrior's Term

Throughout history, armies of all shapes and sizes have awakened to battle at the sound of a war cry, a passionate shout that prepares the heart of a warrior for battle. This warrior term evokes a sense of strength and valor, but also a deep commitment to a cause greater than one's self. You see this when the U.S. Marine Corps shout, "Oorah!" or when fans of the New Orleans Saints chant "Who Dat!" over and over again. From the Florida State Tomahawks' war chant to the rebel yell used by the Confederate soldiers, people all over the world have utilized a war cry without even realizing it.

The Bible is also full of passionate warriors who surrendered to God and unleashed a WarCry that echoed throughout their generations. Don't be fooled; these warriors were not what you might imagine. They were not physically strong, fast, or fearless. Instead, they were passionate, committed, and courageous. In fact, those who accomplished the greatest exploits for God were overwhelmingly normal. Many of them were weak and hesitant. The majority of them had to endure great hardship.

They also had something else in common, a powerful God who identified them as strong when everyone else defined them as weak:

> Gideon was known as a baker, but God saw an earth-shaker.
>
> Jeremiah was a youth, but boldly spoke the truth.
>
> Moses had a stutter, but became a national deliverer.
>
> David was a shepherd who refused to retreat.
>
> Deborah was a judge who arose for battle.
>
> Saul the murderer became Paul the Apostle.
>
> Mary was a simple girl who carried the greatest treasure in all of history.

Jesus was born in a manger, but will return one day as a warrior king.

As a warrior, you also have a WarCry.

The world wants to bully you into silence, because your words are more powerful than you can imagine. But God has strengthened you with His mighty hand and calls you more than a conqueror through Christ Jesus (Romans 8:37).

More Than A Conqueror, A Warrior

In October of 2002, my world changed dramatically, but I had made my choice.

The Sunday morning following my mom's death, I walked into church all by myself, ran straight to the front, and collapsed at the altar. With tears streaming down my face, I had decided to trust God, even though I did not understand. This was the weakest moment of my entire life, but Scripture reveals that, in our weakness, God is our strength.

Upon surrendering, I felt the Lord whisper into my ear something that I will never forget. He simply said, "Do not stay down. Rise up; you are a warrior on My mission in this world."

I can remember asking the Lord to clarify.

After all, I had never killed a giant. I had never walked on water. I had never seen the walls of a grand city come crashing down or witnessed fire fall from heaven. I have not the stature of a soldier, nor the grace of a king. And yet, I just could not shake this word in my heart.

The Lord led me to Joel 3:10: Let the weak say, "I am a warrior" (ESV).

As a 4-foot, 11-inch student from a broken home, this Scripture changed my entire perspective of myself. I realized that no one holds the power to define me, except for God. According to the world I was weak, but in the eyes of God, this was the prerequisite for bearing His strength.

When this message finally settled in, I realized God had not placed me on Earth for pleasure, but for a purpose. Not for complacency, but for victory. God was not calling me to be on mission when I graduated; He was calling me to be on His mission for life.

What God had pressed upon my heart at the death of my mom became real to me more than ever: silence is no longer an option.

My parents had been bullied into silence. My friends had been bullied into silence by the choices they were making and the dead ends they were pursuing. With overwhelming negative media messages and global threats on all fronts, even my generation was being targeted for silence. I decided that day that I would not sit back and remain silent.

Maybe you, or someone you know, has been bullied into silence. Similar to my story, you may be broken and bruised by the cards that life has dealt you. Perhaps you have a God-sized dream growing inside your heart, but every turn is full of obstacles. Or maybe you want to live dangerously, but walls of compromise need to be torn down. Does confusion currently mark your calling? For whatever reason, maybe the fire within your heart has grown dimmer ... but it is not dead.

No person is born with an innate desire to be silent, and no child of God is called to a lifestyle of silence. Inside every person lies a burning desire for more, a warrior spirit to step out and do something extraordinary. If you look deep down in your heart, you know you were created for more than what you give yourself credit for, more than what the world says, and more than what others speak over you.

Your past does not dictate your future, your mistakes do not determine your destiny, and your weaknesses do not hold you down. In Christ, your weakness actually becomes your greatest strength! It is time for the weak to say, "I am a warrior! Not because I am strong, but because I am surrendered."

Arise, warrior; do you hear the Lord calling you to battle? Not a battle against flesh and blood; that victory was already won at the cross. Rather, this is a battle against the forces of darkness currently invading the Earth. In this battle, you win not by being the most skilled in combat; you win by surrendering. When you are weak, God's strength will fight through you. The sword that you wield is not visible, but rather stirs deep inside as the Word of God. This stirring bursts forth in a mighty surge of God's power: a WarCry!

Don't get stuck by simply accepting the average and ordinary when God is calling you to be extraordinary. Yes, you are a student, a leader, a business professional, a parent, but do not be fooled. You are also a warrior. And as a warrior, you have a voice stirring within you to fight back against the silence of a generation.

If the Bible said, "you are a conqueror," that would be awesome. But it does not say this. It actually says that you are *more than a conqueror*, through Christ Jesus (Romans 8:37).

You are more than a conqueror: you are a warrior.

A warrior doesn't just survive; a warrior thrives.

A warrior is dangerous.

A warrior moves forward in the face of tragedy.

A warrior is a brave fighter in the Spirit.

If you are reading this right now, God has placed this message in your hands for such a time as this. There is no doubt in my mind that this generation is set apart for a unique purpose. In fact, what you see as a setback is actually a set up! If you will be patient in the process, God will position you perfectly for His purpose—a purpose that is higher than any person could imagine. A purpose so strategic that hell has sent out an attack of silence to stop you.

But, you are a warrior and every warrior has a WarCry.

An opportunity to march or sit on the sidelines.

To fight or retreat in fear.

To speak or be silent.

For every person tired of playing it safe and living the mundane, ordinary life, this is your wake-up call.

For every person who has a burning dream for something more, this is your mission, should you choose to accept it: to break through the silence of your generation by identifying your authentic voice and unleashing your WarCry.

By turning this page, you are heeding the call to be a modern-day warrior on God's mission in your world.

[2]

Silence Is No Longer an Option

*"Our lives begin to end the day
we become silent about the things that matter."*
~ Martin Luther King Jr.

GOD LOVES TO INTERRUPT the ordinary with the extraordinary.

On one average, ordinary, youth night the Holy Spirit spoke to me in a very extraordinary way. Out of nowhere, I heard Him say one simple word, "Speak."

With greater intensity, I heard the Holy Spirit say once again, "Speak!" An overwhelming feeling came over me, as if my words at that moment would mean the difference between life or death for someone.

So, words began to flow from my mouth as I prayed.

A third time I heard one simple, but very strong word: "Speak!"

I continued to pray, but it was only a few sentences later that my prayers took on a whole different motivation. I began tearing down strongholds of sin and fear, praying for fire, and pleading for my generation. The Holy Spirit flowed through my words as I began to pray in the Spirit. Then, I felt the power of God rise up from within me with the same message, "Speak! Speak! Speak!" Over and over again, this message resonated within my spirit.

I finally accepted that the Holy Spirit was telling me to speak for Him. Not just in that moment, but every day of my life. Not only into a microphone, but also in the secret place, my prayer closet.

From this experience, the Holy Spirit began to coach me on what it means to truly speak. This is a message that would eventually lead me to discover the power of the WarCry. In fact, this was how I first began to break through the silence of my past.

While it is not necessary to be loud, I am now convinced that when we speak the word of God with passion, power, and purpose, something is stirred in the spiritual realm. God begins to work behind the scenes and the atmosphere is transformed. All throughout Scripture, we see men and women of God become passionate and release a mighty WarCry over their situation. While not always a shout, it is characterized by intensity and deeply rooted in a Word from God.

There is something powerful about your words. If the enemy can't take you out or distract you, he will desperately search for a way to silence you. Without your words, you are a weaponless soldier, a muted warrior.

Since the beginning, the enemy has been trying to silence believers. If he can muffle, suppress, or even mute your ability to speak, then he can prevent you from moving forward.

That is why the Word of God is the sword of truth. When you audibly speak God's Word, a spiritual sword is taken up for battle.

Proverbs 18:21 says, *The **tongue** has the power of **life and death**...* (emphasis added).

Life is found in the tongue. What is one major way that the enemy seeks to steal our life? By stealing our words—which hold the power of life!

The enemy wants you and me to walk around as muted warriors, because our words are the most powerful way to break through the silence. As a spiritual warrior speaks the Word, life or death is birthed in the spiritual realm.

The Bible says that from the abundance of the heart we speak (Luke 6:45). Our words are the outward flow of the Holy Spirit, who lives within us. The enemy cannot stop the Holy Spirit moving within us, but he sure does try to clog our hearts with doubt, laziness, and fear so that the Holy Spirit cannot effectively move out from us.

That is why we must stand on the Word of God and declare, "Silence is no longer an option!" Do not be a muted warrior amidst a generation of silence! If only believers everywhere would awaken to the power of their words. Let us learn how to speak into existence the purpose, promises, and potential that Christ has for us!

NO *IFS* WITH GOD

In Mark 9:14–29, Jesus arrives on the scene as a distressed father runs forward with his epileptic son. In verses 17 and 18, the father cries out to Jesus, *"Teacher, I brought my son to you, for he has a spirit that makes him mute. And whenever it seizes him, it throws him down, and he foams and grinds his teeth and becomes* rigid. So I asked your disciples to cast it out, and they were not able" (ESV).

First, we can see that the son was completely silenced by a spirit that made him mute, or unable to speak. We also see that a mute spirit is a very serious issue; not even the disciples were able to free the boy!

What did Jesus say to the man's outcry? He responded in a puzzling way: *"O faithless generation, how long am I to be with you? How long am I to bear with you?"* (v. 19).

Jesus did not instantly heal the boy. Instead, He linked a lack of faith with failure to wage effective spiritual warfare! He was distraught by the fact that the disciples did not have enough faith to cast out the mute spirit. He also explained that some things can only come out through prayer and fasting. This is because we are engaged in a spiritual battle, and so we must fight with spiritual weapons. Prayer, fasting, worship, and the Word are weapons we take up in the fight of faith.

Luckily, in this story, the father understands that in a spiritual battle you must refuse to be silenced by the enemy. Therefore, with urgency, he once again asks Jesus to heal his son from the mute spirit. *"But if you can do anything, have compassion on us and help us"* (v. 22).

This time Jesus fervently replied, *"If you can! All things are possible for one who believes"* (v. 23).

Jesus makes it clear here that there are no "ifs" with God, because through faith all things are possible!

Immediately, the father of the child repented as he cried out, *"I believe; help my unbelief!"* (v. 24).

Press the pause button for a minute and focus on the fact that Scripture says that the father literally *cried out* in this moment. He did the opposite of being quiet or apprehensive.

In fact, the Amplified Version describes the father's outcry in this way: *Immediately the father of the boy cried out [with a desperate, piercing cry], saying, "I do believe; help [me overcome] my unbelief."*

This, my friends, is an example of a WarCry.

The WarCry of a desperate father broke the mute spirit off of his son. This cry *was not* pretty, harmonized, or even completely understandable by those around him, but it *was* passionate, desperate, and understood perfectly by Jesus. How could our Heavenly Father not respond to a desperate cry from one of His children?

A lack of faith can prevent us from unleashing a WarCry, but a declaration made from a heart full of faith ushers in an immediate response from our Lord. Sometimes the response is "yes," other times "no," and sometimes He simply asks us to wait. But rest assured, He will always respond.

It Only Takes One

On September 11, 1297, a bloody battle occurred a Stirling Bridge. The Scottish rebels had finally determined in their hearts to no longer remain silent. The battle at Stirling Bridge was destined to be their great stand for Scottish independence. In the distance, a grand British army five times their size could be seen marching toward the battle line. They were suited in thick war gear, with synchronized steps and long spears. Clearly, this fight was not going to end well for the rebels.

A great silence fell over the troops as they stood outnumbered and hopeless, ready to turn back. The air was heavy with fear as the mighty British soldiers advanced forward, leaving the Scottish rebels with only two options: flee and give up on their quest for independence, or die fighting a lost cause.

In that moment, the Scottish rebels were silent warriors, paralyzed by fear and ready to turn back. But deep down they all still had a reason to fight—**someone just needed to raise their voice and awaken the passion that had been lost.** That person was William Wallace.

Today, nearly every person has heard the famous line Mel Gibson, acting as William Wallace in the movie *Braveheart*, shouted to his soldiers just before they fight the English army: *They may take our lives, but they'll never take our freedom!*

This line is part of the speech that Wallace gave after a fearful soldier suggested they turn back.

At the end of his frenzied rant, Wallace had fired up the army so greatly that they responded with a corporate war cry. In the movie, you can see the passion and confidence building up with the release of each syllable: "Alba gu bráth!" This war cry, translated as "Scotland forever!" was intended to build up the weary soldiers and scare the opposing side. In essence, they were declaring that, no matter the disadvantage, they were going to fight for their freedom. Each time they released the war cry, it unified the soldiers and sent chills through the enemy. In the next scene, the rebel army ran toward the battle line, screaming the war cry, with William Wallace at the front of the pack.

At the end of the Battle of Stirling Bridge, these lowly and outnumbered soldiers did indeed defeat the great British army. Against all odds, their heart and passion won a battle that seemed impossible. This was truly a miracle victory for the rebels.

Maybe you have wondered, like I have, "What if the

rebels had turned back? What if William Wallace had never released the war cry from within?" This battle for Scotland's independence would have never happened, and ultimately, they would have lost the war. Instead, they had a clear vision for why they were fighting and moved forward accordingly.

This is not much different from the WarCry released by the father in Mark 9. Both of these true stories show people that were up against great odds, faced by a serious enemy, and unwilling to back down. The father and the Scottish rebels were both willing to risk their lives for a cause greater than themselves.

I deeply believe that God is looking for soldiers who will, against all odds, risk their lives for a purpose that extends beyond this world. You are meant to be a voice to this broken generation. To stand up like William Wallace and say, "Shake the dirt off your feet, raise your head, and prepare for battle!" To release a personal WarCry and stir others to release theirs. Do you hear the Lord whispering to your heart, "Silence is no longer an option?"

Remember, it only takes one person to stand up.

Although different according to the situation, every war cry serves the same purpose:

> To stir up passion amongst soldiers and prepare hearts for battle.
>
> To inflict intimidation on the opposing side.
>
> To cause the enemy to flee.
>
> It is often used alongside instruments.
>
> It is often preceded by a battle speech.

It is not necessarily articulate, but intensely invokes an emotion.

God used the power of the spoken word to put the Earth and all of the planets into orbit. Many biblical victories were won at the sound of the trumpet and a passionate shout.

The Bible says, *"from the abundance of the heart, the mouth speaks"* (Matthew 12:34, MEV). Our words are the outward flow of the Holy Spirit that resides within us.

Be aware that I am not saying your words are a formula to make God do what you want. Rather, when the Lord drops a word into your heart, we have a responsibility to speak this word into existence.

"I believed, and so I spoke," we also believe, and so we also speak...
~ 2 Corinthians 4:13b, ESV

Because I believe, I speak. In fact, it is my responsibility to speak, because I believe. Releasing a spiritual WarCry requires you to speak! It only takes the voice of one to initiate a revolution.

We are the "Now" Generation

We live in a fallen world and fight a daily battle against forces of darkness. There is an all-out attack on your an entire generations ability to speak the truth of Gods word. The mute spirit is sent directly by the pit of hell to silence humankind. Although a mute spirit cannot overpower and control a Christian, it does set up a fierce attack.

After working in youth ministry for over ten years, I am deeply saddened by the great number of young people who are weighed down, lost, and gagged by the snare of silence.

Many Christians have become desensitized to the power of God's word and its ability to flow through them. Or, like the disciples, their character and spiritual depth are not strong enough to back up the declarations that are spoken. As a result, they grow weary and give up. Both instances are a part of the enemy's plan to steal, kill, and destroy our ability to live an abundant life!

However, if you recall Mark 9:19, Jesus did not say, "...you faithless *disciples*," He said, "...you faithless *generation*."

The attack of the mute spirit is not an individual matter, but a generational matter. The numbers show abortions, suicides, and cyber bullying are at an all time high. The tech-driven Millennial and Centennial generations can spend hours communicating through a device or social network, but have lost the ability to communicate in person. If social media is intended to connect people, why does it seem like more people are being cut off from reality?

Do I use social media? Of course! But there is a problem when social media becomes our only means of connecting to the world, when we are more comfortable with expressing ourselves through a glass screen than to a human face. Sometimes we need to get off Facebook and get on our face before the Lord! How can we expect to cast out evil spirits and function in the supernatural when we cannot hold a face-to-face conversation with another believer?

We live in the time of the "Now" Generation, a title that has been given to those under forty who will be the leaders of tomorrow.

A mute spirit has been forcefully harassing this generation and desperately trying to keep them silenced. If the enemy cannot abort you or lead you to commit suicide, he will do everything he can to silence you.

Why is the attack so strong?

This generation carries a unique anointing and passion that will usher in a mighty move of God, and perhaps even the return of Christ! We cannot be like the disciples, when they did not have enough faith or spiritual depth to move in the anointing of God. Something powerful is happening in the "Now" Generation. God is calling passionate warriors to step out and lead into a new season of revival.

I am calling a generation to step forward and unleash their words into the spirit realm, like mighty bombs being dropped on enemy territory. For too long, we have been the faithless generation that Jesus spoke of in Mark 9. No longer! Let us break out of that mold and show that we are full of faith and ready for battle.

Silence is no longer an option.

[3]

CRY OF A CHAMPION

The LORD will go forth like a warrior,
He will stir up His zeal like a man of war;
He will shout out, yes, He will raise a war cry.
He will prevail [mightily] against His enemies.
~ Isaiah 42:13, AMP

IMAGINE YOU WOKE UP tomorrow morning and, instead of aimlessly reaching for your phone alarm and rolling out of bed, you found yourself completely alert and on a massive battlefield, surrounded by a grand army.

This, however, is not just any army.

As your eyes scan the battlefield, you can't help but notice that every soldier is dressed in all white, including you. The strangest part is that you are about to engage in warfare, but there is no armor to be found. Your gaze curiously moves downward as you notice that you and your fellow riders all sit upon flawless white steeds.

All of a sudden, a noise like you have never heard causes you look towards the heavens just in time to see them split wide open before your very eyes. The skies reveal a radiant white horse and rider. No one can look away as he makes his way to the front of the army.

This mighty leader looks like none you have ever seen before. His head bears many crowns and within his eyes are mighty flames that pierce Heaven and Earth. You become transfixed by the awesomeness of his presence. All of a sudden, your leader opens his mouth and draws out a sharp sword with which to conquer all who oppose you.

A battle is about to begin, and you are not a spectator but a participator. What do you do? Do you choose to run, or do you choose to stand alongside your champion?

One day you will have to answer this question, because this is not an imaginary situation. The question is not "Will it happen?" but rather, "Which side will you be on when it does?"

Take a moment and read Revelation 19:11–16:

> Then I saw heaven opened, and behold, a white horse! The one sitting on it is called Faithful and True, and in righteousness he judges and makes war. His eyes are like a flame of fire, and on his head are many diadems, and he has a name written that no one knows but himself. He is clothed in a robe dipped in blood, and the name by which he is called is The Word of God. And the armies of heaven, arrayed in fine linen, white and pure, were following him on white horses. From his mouth comes a sharp sword with which to strike down the nations, and he will rule them with a rod of iron. He will tread the winepress of the fury of the wrath of God the Almighty. On his robe and on his thigh he has a name written, King of kings and Lord of lords. (ESV, emphasis added)

Let this sink in for a minute, because this will actually happen one day! It may be somewhat different than what John experienced in his vision, but the truth stands that one day all believers will be representing the King of kings and the Lord of lords as He wages war against evil. This is the main event at the end of all days, for which the Church is eagerly awaiting!

In verse 15, we see that Christ is coming back to destroy the enemy of His people. Jesus is our Champion, our conquering King and Almighty Avenger. At His return, Jesus will not come as a baby in a manger, but as a Warrior-Messiah with a grand army! This time, no religious leader or political powerhouse will mistake His identity.

The "armies of Heaven" in verse 14 refers to all of the inhabitants of Earth who are in Heaven. That will hopefully mean you and me! Those who do not find themselves on the side of Jesus Christ will only encounter judgment and defeat. The world will then see Jesus for who He really is and the people of God for who we really are—mighty warriors!

Warrior Ethos

Even though this long-awaited event will take place in the future, it is imperative that we realize that our current actions and behaviors will directly affect where we stand on that day. Will you choose to stand up for God? Don't fail to realize that we are in a real war today:

> *For our struggle is not against flesh and blood, but against the rulers, against the authorities, against the powers of this dark world and against the spiritual forces of evil in the heavenly realms.* ~ Ephesians 6:12

The battle we fight is not for *our* eternity, because Christ already won the war at the cross. Rather, we fight the good fight of faith, becoming more like Christ every day and engaging in spiritual warfare for other people.

Christians can learn something very important from the

U.S. Army. Take a look at the Warrior Ethos that every soldier in the U.S. Army lives by (Scriptures added):

1. **I will always place the mission first.** — *"All authority in heaven and on earth has been given to me. Therefore go and make disciples of all nations, baptizing them in the name of the Father and of the Son and of the Holy Spirit, and teaching them to obey everything I have commanded you."* ~ Matthew 28:18b–20

2. **I will never accept defeat.** — *"Have I not commanded you? Be strong and courageous. Do not be afraid; do not be discouraged, for the LORD your God will be with you wherever you go."* ~ Joshua 1:9

3. **I will never quit.** — *Therefore, since we are surrounded by such a great cloud of witnesses, let us throw off everything that hinders and the sin that so easily entangles. And let us run with perseverance the race marked out for us, fixing our eyes on Jesus, the pioneer and perfecter of faith.* ~ Hebrews 12:1–2a

4. **I will never leave a fallen comrade.** — *So speak encouraging words to one another. Build up hope so you'll all be together in this, no one left out, no one left behind. I know you're already doing this; just keep on doing it.*
~ 1 Thessalonians 5:11, MSG

I firmly believe that this world needs some Kingdom warriors who will apply the Warrior Ethos to spiritual battle. One such warrior was Cassie Bernall.

An Unshakable Stand

Cassie woke up in her Colorado home the morning of April 20, 1999, just like she did every other school day. She was one of those students who always wore the "Talk to me about Jesus" T-shirt and spent her lunch hour ministering to her classmates. With the WWJD bracelet around her wrist and a Bible in her hand, you would probably catch Cassie at a Christian club or hanging out at her youth group on Wednesday nights.

In fact, two days earlier, Cassie had even built up the courage to share her testimony with her youth group. She boldly shared about her previous involvement in witchcraft, but that Christ had changed her life and now there was no way she could live without Him.

However, Cassie's life was cut short on that fateful day when another student held 17-year-old Cassie at gunpoint in the library of Columbine High School.

"Do you believe in God?" The gunman demanded.

Knowing that one answer would save her life and the other would take it, Cassie did the bravest thing any Christian could do.

Other students remember a hesitation in her voice as she counted down the final moments to her death. Cassie's response was a scared, but strong, "Yes."

"Why?" was all he asked, just before pulling the trigger.

Cassie knew her Father's heart, and she had heard His cry. This led her to take an unshakable stand and boldly proclaim the name of Jesus, not only with her words, but also with her actions.

War cries have stirred young people to fight for a variety of causes. However, our cry is much different than that of the world. We are not fighting for territory or rights; we are fighting for people.

Like Cassie, a true champion knows where their strength lies. It is not ability, but rather heart, that defines their strength.

The strength of a champion is always grounded in love. God so loved the world that He sent His son to die so our sins could be forgiven (John 3:16).

In all of God's awesomeness, He has chosen us, not because we are strong, but because He loves us.

No person in my life has the heart of a champion more than my husband. I prayed for an Italian with green eyes, and, before I knew it, there he was. Joe tries so hard to never show favoritism or look down upon someone else. He is the most encouraging person I know, and whether you are a Bible scholar, hobo, or student, he will make you feel like the world-changer you are. You should see his eyes glisten when he hears testimonies of young people doing passionate exploits for the Lord. You see, love is always the greatest motivation of a true champion.

If I have a faith that can move mountains, but do not have love, I am nothing (1 Corinthians 13:2b). It is a sobering truth that we are nothing without love. God could finish writing His own story, but because He is motivated by love, He actually wants us to be a part of writing history. Our champion wants His Church to be presented without stain at the end of all time. It is love, expressed as the heart of a Father, that motivates everything that God does.

Cassie understood this. Following her death at Columbine High School, a verse from Philippians 3 was found recorded in her journal. It was the last thing she had written before she met Jesus.

Now I have given up on everything else—I have found it to be the only way to really know Christ and to experience the mighty power that brought Him back to life again and to find out what it means to suffer and die with Him. So, whatever it takes I will be the one who lives in the fresh newness of life of those who are alive from the dead.

~ Philippians 3:10-11, TLB

Cassie Bernall was a brave warrior who courageously advanced the Kingdom of Heaven. Her love for God and love for her friends led her to make the greatest sacrifice a person can make. She was willing to lay down her life for her faith. As a result, the following weeks at Columbine High School were filled with revival.

How will you take a stand for Christ? God does not ask all of us to die for Him; in fact, He asks the majority of us to live for Him—completely sold out and on fire with passion for His cause.

The opposite of silence is *loud noise*—a WarCry. Let us learn to break through the silence with a mighty WarCry that shakes the nations and causes the armies of God to take a stand for the one true King.

With a Shout

With a shout he will raise the battle cry and will triumph over his enemies. ~ Isaiah 42:13

Scripture doesn't say exactly what God's WarCry is, only that He has one and He does not whisper it. On the contrary, He shouts it! This shout leads Him to triumph over his enemies.

The more we can understand God's WarCry, the better we understand the WarCry that God has uniquely placed deep within us. Be cautious in this process, because everyone wants to be a hero, but the truth is that God is the only champion. He is the mighty warrior. He is the hero. Just read the stories of King David, Joshua at Jericho, Daniel in the lion's den, Queen Esther, or the resurrection of Jesus—they all testify to the fact that God is a mighty champion who avenges those who obey Him wholeheartedly.

Throughout history, an army would send out their strongest champion first to strike fear into the enemy. God is the champion who marches out and triumphs over our enemies. He is also our rear guard to protect us from behind.

God is the ultimate hero, but it is mind-blowing that He calls us to take part in His eternal mission. He has chosen us to fight alongside Him for our generation, because He loves us and He wants to work through us. This is an honor and a privilege, not a right that we receive simply because we attend church.

The Bible says we are created in God's image (Genesis 1:27); therefore, we too can be champions. God is calling you to be a chain-breaker, a mountain-mover, and a history-maker, but we must have the heart of a champion in all we do. Please take this to heart:

> *Just like Cassie, you are not just an average student, businessperson, or college student; you are a warrior. When you walk through the hallways of your campus, home, or workplace, you do not just carry a backpack; you wield a spiritual sword. You don't just hold a pencil; you wield the Word of God.*

For too long, Christians have watched silently as the enemy has advanced on our territory. For too long, our schools and communities been lulled to sleep by the tunes of abortion, addiction, and pride. No longer! The Lord is calling His Church to hear His cry: *The LORD roars from Zion, and utters his voice from Jerusalem, and the heavens and the earth quake. But the LORD is a refuge to his people, a stronghold to the people of Israel* (Joel 3:16, ESV).

The Lord shouts as a roaring lion with a booming voice that causes the heavens and earth to tremble at His word. Do you hear God's mighty shout calling you to stand for Him? Do you sense His passion calling you to respond to His voice?

Understand that God, as our Champion, has been raising a WarCry since the beginning of time. We must first awaken to His voice before we can unleash our own. It is my prayer that you hear the wake-up call:

> *And do this, understanding the present time: The hour has already come for you to wake up from your slumber, because our salvation is nearer now than when we first believed. The night is nearly over; the day is almost here. So let us put aside the deeds of darkness and put on the armor of light.* ~ Romans 13:11–12

It is time for a wounded army to awaken and stand unified against the forces of darkness with God as our Champion.

PART 1

WARCRY OF A LEADER

[4]

WIDE AWAKE

> *"The soldier is summoned to a life of active duty and so is the Christian."*
> ~ William Gurnall

IN THE FALL OF 2004, four hurricanes sped across the Atlantic Ocean with the little state of Florida on their radar. Hitting our state in a matter of consecutive months, Charley, Frances, Ivan, and Jeanne left us in utter chaos.

At least my "senioritis" that year was lessened by the fact that schools were closed more than they were open. On the down side, we were trapped inside our homes for what felt like an entire year. Power became a luxury and sleepovers a necessity, without which we all would have gone completely mad.

One might think that multiple weeks off of school would make for the best senior year ever, but after a few weeks it felt like we were prisoners in our own homes.

Fortunately, my senior year was not a total loss. I was able to attend school for eight of the ten months of the school year, and I walked away with a senior t-shirt that read, "We survived 2005" above a weather chart of four massive hurricanes encircling Florida.

There is nothing worse than feeling trapped. Whether you are stuck in a dating relationship or imprisoned in your own home by a hurricane, everyone cringes at the thought of being trapped. Feelings of suffocation and isolation sink in as you are cut off from everything you knew to be normal. The fear becomes overwhelming as you wonder, "Can anyone hear me?"

It may be hard to imagine, but what if you were permanently trapped? You tried to scream, but no one could hear you. You tried to break free, but invisible chains held you down. Does this sound like something out of a Sherlock Holmes movie? I wish it were.

You know that place between asleep and awake? Where your surroundings are hazy, but all other senses are on high alert? It was in this state that I found myself trapped in every sense of the word. My body was completely frozen, but my mind was wide-awake and could make out the hazy outline of my bedroom. I tried to scream, but no words came out. I wrestled inside my mind, trying to wake up. My throat felt like it was painfully glued shut as I was trapped to my own bed, unable to make a sound. After fighting for what seemed like hours, even though it was probably only one minute, something caused me to wake up.

Looking back, I knew that this night terror was an attack, but sadly, I was a silent warrior, unable to stand up against the enemy. I had no voice. My WarCry was completely muted by fear as enemy forces surrounded me.

Do you want to know the sad truth? I thought I was a strong

Christian. I went to church every week, took communion, and raised my hands in worship. I prayed hard in human video practice and even gave up hanging out with all my non-Christian friends that were pulling me away from Christ. However, the enemy had wound me up so tightly that I was inwardly suffocating to death.

This may be an extreme example of what happens when a warrior is silent, but unfortunately this a reality for many believers. They are saved, but silenced— deeply wounded and falling short of their full potential. This was me, I was missing a voice, my WarCry. By the end of my senior year it became glaringly apparent that I didn't survive 2005 as well as I thought I had.

Suddenly everything became crystal clear. The majority of my family—aunts, uncles, grandparents, and even cousins— were all chained to an addiction or disease of some kind. Both sides of my family were caught up in alcoholism, gambling, overspending, and drug abuse. As a new believer, my spiritual eyes were awakened to the addiction and disease that was running rampant in my family.

Even though I was saved and living for God, I too was unequipped to fight the good fight of faith. I was a silent warrior, and it was time for me wake up and unleash my voice.

Desperate and Determined

It's 6:15 a.m.

Your alarm clock goes off the way it does every morning, and you hit the snooze button the way you do every morning. Your heavy eyelids begin to close, and your heart drops as you realize ... it is time to wake up.

What if today was different? Instead of complaining about

the day to come, you choose to think, "Perhaps today will be a day of divine destiny. Something may happen today that will change my entire life forever."

These were the words I fought to tell myself every morning of my high school years, often through tears. Being diagnosed with hypothyroidism at the age of eighteen didn't give me back the years I had spent not realizing I was sick. Having Hypothyroidism meant that I lacked an essential hormone needed for the normal function of virtually every organ in the body.

Those four years of high school had left me burdened with horrible pain. My brain was in a continual fog and waking up in the morning was the greatest obstacle I faced each day.

With the diagnosis came negative thoughts that filled my mind with the enemies lies. *You will have to take a pill every day for the rest of your life! You will never be able to do what you want to do or be who you want to be!*

But God had a different plan.

I began to seek the Lord with great desperation and study the Scriptures more intensely than I ever had before.

Every Sunday, I would dwell in the presence of God after church at the altar. I stayed up late at night seeking God's face in my personal Bible study. It was not always about the length of time spent in prayer, but rather the desperation that marked my prayers.

One night, God woke me up with a burning sensation all down my throat and through my left hand. As overwhelming peace flooded my body, I just knew that something was about to change. The next morning, I awoke full of strength and life for the first time since I was a child. No pain, sickness, or weariness.

For the first time in years, my throat was opened and I could speak clearly. I felt like I had been sleeping for twenty-one years and, in that moment, I was finally wide awake. God had completely healed me from the hypothyroidism and I never experienced a night terror again. All glory to God!

And do this, understanding the present time: The hour has already come for you to wake up from your slumber, because our salvation is nearer now than when we first believed. ~ Romans 13:11

What does this Scripture mean when it says "wake up from slumber?" If you have not guessed, it refers to so much more than what happens when your alarm clock goes off and you want to hit the snooze button. It refers to waking up from spiritual sleep, sickness, and even death! It means gaining the strength to *stand up* out of a place of slumber and literally arise out of the darkness that once held you down.

Many Christians are silent because they are spiritually asleep. It would be fair to say that our generation is a sleeping giant. We are being lulled to sleep by immorality, insecurity, and disunity.

Our generation is oozing with creativity, innovation, and power! When will the sleeping giant awaken and prepare for battle? When will our generation stand up out of their spiritual death, sickness, and slumber? God is calling us to understand the times we live in, and awaken our WarCry and fight!

What wakes us up from spiritual sleep? Desperation. To wake up, we must become desperate and determined to seek the face of God. We must become desperate for intimacy with the Father. Intimacy simply means having a deep, genuine relationship with someone. This close relationship with God is the only way that we will rise up out of our slumber.

I am not saying that this is the formula for healing; I am saying that, in my situation, desperation for the Lord was the key to *my* healing.

The Bible says, *By his stripes (wounds) we are healed* (Isaiah 53:5, AMP). Not in our strength, but by His grace we are healed. In this instance, the Lord was teaching me something very important: God's face is turned toward those who desperately seek to be close to Him.

One of my favorite stories revolves around Zacchaeus, a vertically-challenged tax collector who became so desperate to get a glimpse of Jesus that he climbed a nearby sycamore tree (Luke 19). This was no easy task for a man of small stature, who was likely business clothes. But verse three tells us that *[Zacchaeus] wanted desperately to see Jesus* (MSG)—so much so that he was willing to do whatever it took to get just a glimpse of Jesus's face.

When Zacchaeus started to climb that tree, he made a decision to move against the flow of the crowd and step out of the status quo. He set aside his reputation, his past, and his fear of what other people might think of him. Desperate people do desperate things, and Zacchaeus was both desperate and determined.

After climbing the giant sycamore tree, Zacchaeus was spotted by Jesus—even in the midst of the mob of people. The next thing Zacchaeus knew, he was being invited to dinner with Jesus! Sharing food with someone is very intimate business. This story reveals that godly desperation results in an encounter with Jesus. I'll bet Zacchaeus woke up that morning, saying to himself, "Today will be different. Today will be a day of divine destiny and purpose. Something will happen today that will change my entire life forever."

And something did happen: Zacchaeus had an encounter with Jesus.

If we want to awaken to God's presence, we must get desperate and determined to seek His face. This leads us to step out and sound an alarm to awaken others to His presence. This, my friends, is the WarCry of a leader. It is not something that is forced, but rather an overflow from our desperation.

Fearless Leader: Tilly's Story

10 Year Old Girl Saves Dozens From Tsunami! This was the headline of the Sun newspaper in January of 2005. All over the world, Tilly Smith was hailed a hero.[1]

Tilly and her family were vacationing on the beautiful Maikhao Beach in Thailand when, all of a sudden, the sea began to bubble. Everyone rushed forward to admire the water, but 10-year-old Tilly stepped back in alarm. The Sun records that Tilly distinctly said, "Mummy, we must get off the beach now! I think there's going to be a tsunami!"[2]

Initially, the adults didn't listen to Tilly. She ran back and forth across the beach shouting a desperate cry from the top of her lungs, "Get to safety! Get off the beach now!"[3] Though no one listened, Tilly was desperate and determined.

The adults finally began to catch on, and within seconds Tilly's warning raced up and down the beach. Everyone escaped the shoreline just seconds before the sea crashed ashore with brutal force, turning the beach and resort to rubble.

The tsunami claimed 230,000 lives along the coast of southeast Asia that day, but not one person on Maikhao Beach was injured.

That day, Tilly Smith was nothing less than a hero. She was

a leader who fearlessly led the people around her to safety.

Tilly recalls, "When the water went back, I was like most people on the beach. I wanted to walk down and look at what was going on."[4] But something inside Tilly triggered an alarm. In that moment, she made the brave decision to follow the voice in her heart, rather than the crowd. As a result, she released a cry that saved the everyone on the beach that day.

The WarCry of a leader is a cry of genuine desperation that says, "Nothing else is more important to me than my relationship with the Lord!" This is birthed out of a desperation to lead people away from danger and toward the saving grace of God, no matter the cost. Tilly's cry was a desperate plea to alert the people on the beach that danger was headed their way.

The Bible says, *I cannot be silent! For I hear the sound of the trumpet, the alarm of war* (Jeremiah 4:19, ESV).

As believers, it is our responsibility to awaken to God's presence and sound the alarm for others to awaken as well.

I firmly believe that, had no one listened to Tilly, she would have continued screaming, even up to the point that the tsunami would have taken them all, herself included.

What Tilly's parents didn't know was her teacher taught her class about earthquakes and how the water begins to bubble right before a tsunami. Tilly had spent an entire semester learning about tsunamis and earthquakes. So, in one of the most important moments of her young life, she was ready. Tilly had been prepared for this moment!

After we have been prepared in the secret place, then we are ready to step into our divine destiny. It's difficult to do great exploits for God without first knowing what God wants you to say and do—this is only discovered by prayer and intimacy with the Lord. Your WarCry is birthed in prayer and intercession.

The greatest social network is not Facebook, Twitter, or Instagram ... it is prayer! The best part is that God will never 'like' or 'dislike' your post. He will never judge or ridicule you. You will never take Him by surprise or confuse Him. And, no matter what you do, He will never love you less or leave you high and dry.

Every believer is a leader, because we have been given the responsibility to lead others to Christ. Like Tilly, you can become a fearless leader that releases a WarCry ten times your size.

Right now, lives hang in the balance between life and death. You have the ability to sound the alarm; to release the WarCry of a leader and awaken others to God's presence.

[5]

ARISE FOR BATTLE

*"The warrior is not someone who fights,
because no one has the right
to take another life. The warrior, for us, is one
who sacrifices himself for the good of others."*
~ Sitting Bull

IMAGINE A BATTLEFIELD WITH two opposing armies preparing to face off. One side stands the mighty Canaanites! Their army consists of 300,000 footmen, 10,000 horsemen, and 900 hundred chariots of iron (which would have been like tanks in modern day America).

On the opposing side are the Israelites!

This group of rag-tag warriors is not what one would normally consider to be an army of soldiers, but they are desperate for freedom. Led by the prophetess Deborah and General Barak, the Israelites are weaponless and far outnumbered ... but don't count them out of the battle yet!

They should not be underestimated, because this group of misfits has a secret weapon the enemy is not aware of. They have a sniper who never misses the mark.

Snipers are often the most feared warriors on the battlefield. They are quiet, stealthy, and go unseen by most. Not only are they practically invisible, snipers are excellent marksmen and rarely, if ever, do they miss the target. Pinpoint accuracy renders their shots perfect, even from a great distance. Their long-range rifles are equipped with suppressors, meant to block all noise that would usually erupt from a gunshot. They are quiet, skilled, and deadly.

Christians can learn quite a bit from these warriors. In fact, one of the first lessons for a sniper is not to waste bullets—every shot must hit its target!

In the midst of a spiritual battle, God raises up Kingdom warriors who excel as prayer snipers. These individuals do great damage to enemy territory. Prayer snipers are elite marksmen who never waste bullets, because they never miss the target. Their prayers silently penetrate the strongest forces of darkness. Prayer snipers are men and women who are quiet [in that they never seek attention or accolades] but are deadly to the enemy.

Prayer snipers always win in battle, even though they often go unnoticed. This is due to the fact that they are deeply passionate about seeing the Lord's plan accomplished through desperate, hell-pounding, Earth-shaking prayer.

The prayer of the righteous is powerful and effective.
~ James 5:16, NRSV

Never underestimate the power of a prayer sniper!

FROM PALM TREE TO BATTLE LINE

Deborah, spiritual leader and judge over Israel, was the prayer sniper during a time when the Israelites were held captive by the mighty Canaanites.

However, the Canaanite army had no idea that Deborah had spent years sitting under the Palm of Deborah, appropriately named after her, seeking the face of God and interceding with perfect accuracy for the children of Israel. Her prayers were weakening the enemy's armor before they even knew she existed.

Now, take a look at Judges 4:4–5: *Now Deborah, a prophetess, the wife of Lappidoth, was judging Israel at that time. She used to sit under the palm of Deborah between Ramah and Bethel in the hill country of Ephraim, and the people of Israel came up to her for judgment* (ESV).

I'm convinced if Deborah were alive today, she would live in Florida. This palm-tree lover didn't mind spending a significant amount of time dwelling in God's presence, because she understood this important truth: It takes only a few moments with God to change the course of history forever.

As Deborah sat under the palm tree, God was preparing her in the secret place. Quietly, she was abiding in the Lord and establishing herself in His presence. During this time, I bet that God began to download into Deborah's heart strategic war plans for victory against an impossible foe.

Then, in Judges chapter 4, God tells Deborah to have General Barak lead an army against the evil Canaanite army.

Barak, afraid and doubtful, refuses to go to battle unless Deborah goes with him.

Then, something powerful takes place.

In verse nine, the Bible says something simple, yet so profound: *Then Deborah arose* (ESV).

After years of prayer and intercession, God said, "Deborah,

it is time to arise for war!"

In that moment, Deborah had a choice.

As she stood up for war, she did not arise in the strength of her ministry, degree, personality, or family status; she stood up that day in the strength of the Lord! I believe leagues of angels stood up with her in the spirit realm, far outnumbering the opposing side.

Deborah went from under a palm tree to the battle line in the blink of an eye.

The enemy came to battle with swords and chariots. Deborah came to battle with a different type of weapon. In her moment of crisis, Deborah declared the Word of the Lord over her situation, and all creation obeyed her command. She had complete faith that her God would give them the victory, and He did! In fact, you should read Judges 5, and see how God gave them the victory that day—I'm not going to spoil all of the details for you!

A Season of Silence

Rewind a decade or so from the great battle of Canaan vs. Israel. At this time, Deborah would not have been found under a tree, but rather in the recesses of a deep, dark temple.

This is because Deborah's role prior to becoming the fourth judge of Israel was most likely that of a lamplighter. This meant it was her job to continuously fill the temple lamps with oil in order to keep them burning for the priests. She would have spent long hours dwelling in the temple, probably praying and interceding for the children of Israel in the darkness of God's holy place.

Deborah was being prepared in the secret place. She knew that sincere and passionate prayer was the key to unlocking her relationship with the Lord. This was Deborah's season of silence. God was preparing her to be a prayer sniper and battle hero. She spent hours locked away in the temple, tending to the lamps.

Do not be confused. Am I telling you now to be silent? Yes, but only during the season in which God calls you to be silent! Here is the key to understanding your season of silence:

1. Know when to be silent and when to speak.
2. Know who is asking you to be silent. The Lord asks you to be silent for a season so He can prepare you, while the world and the enemy tells you to be silent so they can compromise you. Make sure you know the difference.
3. The season of silence is a time of preparation ordained by God.

There is a time and a place for everything in God's Kingdom—even a season to speak and a season to be silent (Ecclesiastes 3).

In discovering and developing your WarCry, it is essential to realize that every person whom God uses mightily must first go through a season of silence, a season of preparation where God begins to remove wrong thought patterns, emotions, and poor discipline from your life. This season usually involves a time where you must serve and seek the face of God, despite opposition from people.

The very first opportunity I had in ministry was not teaching, ushering, or leading people. It was serving in a part of my youth ministry known as "CREW."

This was a fairly small team with the task of setting up and tearing down for weekly youth services. With the youth ministry consisting of over 1,000 students, this was no easy task! For an entire year, I showed up regularly to organize chairs, put up curtains, and unroll tarps ... and then, later that night, turn around and re-stack chairs, take down curtains, and roll up the tarps. This was a preparation season that God orchestrated in my life. I did not have a title, microphone, or influence. What I did have was a broom, two arms, and a joyful spirit (most of the time).

How you respond to your season of silence will greatly determine when and how God uses you later on. Be faithful in serving and seeking the face of God during the season of silence. Then, when God tells you to shout, you will raise your voice, and it won't be you, but God speaking through you! He will take you from the prayer front to the war front in the blink of an eye and will give you unbelievable opportunities to serve Him in mighty ways.

The WarCry of a leader is developed in the season of silence. But be aware: when God tells you, "It's time to arise," you had better be ready to get up and go!

Deborah's Cry

In Scripture, one word that describes a war cry is *teruah*. This means *a shout or a blast of war* in the form of *a shout of alarm or joy*.

As you release the WarCry of a leader, we sound the alarm for war and declare to the world, "Wake up to the presence of the Lord!"

Even as a young believer, you are perfectly positioned to be a leader: *Don't let anyone look down on you because you are young, but set an example for the believers in speech, in conduct, in love, in faith and in purity* (1 Timothy 4:12).

Regardless of your age or background, you are a leader on God's mission to your world. However, with great opportunity comes great responsibility.

God is calling Deborahs to awaken—men and women who will seek the face of God and advance the Kingdom through the power of prayer. After all, battles are won on the prayer front before they are won on the war front! Remember, even though God has already won the ultimate battle against Satan, people's lives hang in the balance. For this reason, the Lord spoke to my heart that the WarCry of a leader is a desperate call to deeper intimacy with God. It is an alarm to nearby armies that need to wake up and be prepared for what the Lord is doing.

God had specifically called Deborah to awaken to His presence, arise for battle, and attack the enemies of God.

Judges 5:12 (ESV) gives a song recounting this epic battle:

"Awake, awake, Deborah! Awake, awake, break out in a song. Arise, Barak, lead away your captives, O son of Abinoam."

After the battle, Deborah and General Barak broke out in a song, but this was no ordinary song; it was a battle song.

Deborah's war cry woke up the armies of the Lord and motivated them to win a battle that was unwinnable in the flesh. This was possible because her shout was birthed out of deep desperation for God's presence. In this busy world, how many leaders do you know who spend a significant amount of time just sitting in the presence of God?

Deborah was one such leader, and this enabled her to be a mouthpiece to her generation and a war hero in battle. Deborah was truly a spiritual leader in her generation.

She understood that Daniel 11:32 (ASV) is still true today:

*...the people that **know their God** shall be strong and do exploits* (emphasis added). Wow, you need to write that down, highlight it, circle it, or something, because it is a great reminder that God calls the weak to be warriors!

This Scripture reveals the key to being strong: knowing God. Let's look at another remarkable modern-day example of releasing the WarCry of a leader to awaken a generation.

The War Cry Leader: Roy Costner

As Liberty High School's valedictorian, Roy Costner was faced with an obstacle when he was told that prayer was no longer allowed at graduation. This courageous student decided to turn this limitation into an opportunity when he ripped apart his pre-approved speech and decided to deliver the Lord's Prayer instead.

The entire student body cheered as Costner boldly recited the Lord's Prayer at his graduation. On that day, Roy Costner made history at his school and will be forever remembered as the guy who refused to remain silent in the face of opposition.

You and I are a part of the Lord's army, and God wants us to make history in our generation. We are the Church, fighting on Earth's battlefield. The blueprint for our victory is found in desperate, earth-shaking, wall-crumbling, and demon-fleeing prayer! The early Church advanced through prayer. Satan is driven back by prayer. The battle for souls is won in prayer.

That is why we need to be like Deborah, and become a people of prayer. Rather than seeking opportunity, Deborah sought God. As a result, people and opportunity came to her.

In the same way, let us hear the alarm of war, awaken to God's presence, and arise for battle in our generation.

How can you arise and make a difference in this world? Before you answer this question, let's discuss how you can protect yourself from the fiery darts of the enemy by declaring, "No trespassing!"

[6]

No Trespassing

> *Jerusalem will be a sacred city, posted:*
> *"NO TRESPASSING."*
> ~ Joel 3:17b MSG

IT IS NOT EVERY day that you visit your mother in jail.

I walked into the dark, strange room, sat in a cold chair, and peered hesitantly through the glass. On the other side was a familiar face.

Sadly, my mom's life of compromise started small with cigarettes, but it wasn't long before she became completely addicted to drugs. I vaguely remember her describing the moment that she tried painkillers for the first time.

As a teenager, she was hospitalized for weeks because of a back problem. Just as the painkillers began flowing into her system via an IV, she recalled, "At that moment I knew I would need the drugs for the rest of my life."

One small area of compromise eventually became so overwhelming that it caused her to lose everything, including her own life.

I tell you this story as a warning. Not to scare you, but to awaken you to the truth that, when you give in to compromise, even something small and unsuspecting, it will eventually take you down.

This is why it is imperative to learn how to declare, "No trespassing" to any area of compromise in our lives.

Take a look at Joel 3:15–17 (MSG):

> *The sky turns black,*
>   *sun and moon go dark, stars burn out.*
> *GOD roars from Zion, shouts from Jerusalem.*
>   *Earth and sky quake in terror.*
> *But GOD is a safe hiding place,*
>   *a granite safe house for the children of Israel.*
> *Then you'll know for sure*
>   *that I'm your GOD,*
> *Living in Zion,*
>   *my sacred mountain.*
> *Jerusalem will be a sacred city, posted: "NO TRESPASSING."*

I am tired of watching the enemy gain ground in the lives of believers simply because they are unable to recognize the attack of the enemy. Let us spiritually hold up a sign and declare that we are the temple of the Holy Spirit, and the enemy cannot trespass in our lives.

These are some areas where the enemy may attack you the hardest:

1. **You can be good without God.**

One flaming arrow the enemy is constantly releasing over this generation is the lie that you can be good without God. In fact, this is the leading vision statement for the Secular Student Alliance, a national organization that recruits high school students to be a part of the atheist, agnostic, humanistic, and free-thought movement.

What this organization fails to realize is Jesus says: "Without me, you can't do anything" (John 15:5b, CEB).

The world says you can be good without God, but God says that only in our weakness do we become strong. Only when we completely surrender is God's power activated in our lives. No one will ever be good enough to deserve God's love, and "good works" do not get us into Heaven! Therefore, the ultimate goal is not even to be "good," but to be surrendered.

When the enemy attacks you with this lie, it is your responsibility to declare *no trespassing*. Here are some Scriptures you can declare over yourself, your family, and your friends:

> *I can do all things through Christ who gives me strength.*
> ~ Philippians 4:13
>
> *He who began a good work in me will be faithful to complete it.*
> ~ Philippians 1:6
>
> *Nothing can ever separate me from the love of God in Christ Jesus.*
> ~ Romans 8:38-39

2. *Blindsided by Busyness.*

If the enemy cannot steal, kill, or destroy you spiritually, he will seek to make us busy. Many people fall into compromise simply because they do not prioritize time with God.

Social media, television, and work all fight for our attention, but the one most deserving of our attention is God. While these other things are not bad, they must be balanced. Do not get so caught up in day-to-day obligations that you lose track of your true purpose! Constantly awaken yourself to what God is doing.

In order to defend yourself against this attack prioritize your relationship with the Lord. The answer is simple, but not always easy to put into practice.

Here are some helpful steps:

- *Spend time before work or school reading the Bible and doing devotions.*
- *Pray daily.*
- *Worship to at least one of your favorite worship songs every day.*

3. Spiritual Suicide by Relationships.

Surrounding yourself with poor relationships may lead to spiritual suicide, because it will rob you of your purity. Whether it is a dating relationship or a friendship, the people surrounding you can lead to your demise if they lead you to compromise.

Unfortunately, *purity* is a lost and forgotten word in our society. Being pure is seen as overrated and weak. In a world consumed by false images of love, how is a believer supposed to remain pure, or even regain their purity?

The Church is overflowing with materials, books, resources, sermons, and counseling for relationship problems—yet this sin still runs rampant in our youth ministries, schools, and homes. While there is a time and a place for all of these wonderful resources, I do not believe the answer to relational suicide is found in another book or a sermon; the answer is found *on your face!*

The real issue here is not one of purity any more than it is an issue of *priority*. When God is first, everything else will work itself out. When you spend time actually praying and seeking the face of God, you won't want to do anything that would hurt Him.

Maintaining uncompromised intimacy in a world of compromise is no easy task. The world may be falling apart before our very eyes, but God says that His people will be a sacred city with a sign posted "No trespassing."

Look at what MTV has publicly proclaimed about the Millennial generation:

> The strongest appeal you can make is emotionally. If you can get their emotions going, make them forget their logic, you've got them. At MTV, we don't shoot for the 14-year-olds; we own them.

Does this wake-up something inside of your spirit? Does it make you desperate for Jesus in a world marked by silence?

It does for me!

I have come to realize that our country struggles with more than just an image problem—we are under an identity crisis and immediate action is needed if we are to recover. We need to learn to say to the enemy, "No trespassing in my life!"

Warrior, not only do you have authority to stop the enemy from trespassing in your lives, you are empowered to trespass on the enemy's camp and take back everything he has stolen from you. It is time to invade the darkness with the light of Christ.

INVADE THE DARKNESS

With nothing but the words "be strong and courageous" echoing in his mind, Joshua prepared the Israelites for battle—if a "battle" is what you wish to call it. Invading and invading Jericho was no easy task. Up against mighty men of valor who were defended by a wall as high as thirty feet and almost equally thick, the Israelites were convinced that only God Himself could win this battle. With eyes fixed on the prize and each stride only growing stronger, the once-captive children of Israel marched proudly on behalf of their God.

Then the moment arrived.

Young Joshua took his final stand before the grand walls of Jericho, completely undaunted by what might be hiding on the other side. Boasting swordsmen, medieval snipers, and the church choir, the Israelite army prepared to march their final steps around the heavily fortified city of Jericho.

In this moment, I wonder if leagues of angels surrounded the battlefield. After all, the commander of the Lord's armies had just appeared to Joshua one chapter earlier! In any case, one thing was for sure: the Israelites were tired of being silent.

Full of excitement, the Lord's army advanced to release their war cry. This declaration of God's victory would be so loud and impactful that not even the gates of Hell would be able to stand against it.

Picture this scene with me as you read Joshua 6:20 (CEB, emphasis added): *Then the people shouted. They blew the trumpets. As soon as the people heard the trumpet blast,* **they shouted a loud war cry.** *Then the wall collapsed.*

I can envision even the smallest soldier mustering up every ounce of energy after walking the length of 84 ½ football fields in seven days. Then, the moment arrived and it was time to shout. Joshua led them in releasing the WarCry of a leader as he called the people to awaken to God's presence and rise up to change their world.

Releasing a war cry was quite common amongst the armies

of Joshua's day, but this was a unique situation. Normally, an army would release a war cry with the hope of inspiring each other and deterring the enemy, but no one up to this point had ever seen a victory won by a simple shout. We must not forget that the Israelites were not a normal army. By faith, they released a war cry, knowing full well that they could not physically bust down the giant wall standing before them.

> *By faith the walls of Jericho fell down, after they were compassed about seven days.* ~ Hebrews 11:30, ASV

The Israelites faithfully obeyed God's word to encircle the city of Jericho for seven days, covering it in prayer. Then, full of faith, they declared God's promises as they released a war cry over the city that God had destined for them to invade. They not only declared, "no trespassing" to the enemy; they trespassed on enemy territory and took back all that the enemy had stolen from them.

In our generation, I'm tired of seeing the Church take a defensive position when she was born to go forth and conquer. God has not commissioned believers to play defensive, but to take their place on the offensive line.

God has created you to conquer. He has strengthened you to invade the enemy's camp. In fact, Matthew 11:12 (AMP) proves we are meant to take an offensive position in spiritual warfare: *And from the days of John the Baptist until the present time, the kingdom of heaven has endured violent assault, and violent men seize it by force [as a precious prize].*

We will not simply waltz up to the gates of Heaven after living a life of complacent worship and dull passion. Our heavenly inheritance is a precious prize that we will gain as a result of running our race with patient endurance and active persistence.

Do you seek and stand for God with ardent zeal and intense exertion? The Kingdom of God is advancing and we need forceful disciples who will carry the Kingdom on their shoulders.

So, when will we stop playing church and actually be the Church? We are an army, destined to storm the gates of Hell and take on mission impossible because ... *the kingdom of God does not consist of talk but of power* (1 Cor. 4:20, ESV). Ultimately, we should be walking, talking, and breathing dynamite for Jesus! When we are locked and loaded with the Word of God, there is nothing that can stand against us. A surrendered believer who knows how to wield the power of God's word within them is a force to be reckoned with.

I can imagine the Israelite army, made up of ordinary people, equipped with virtually nothing, and up against a foe secured behind a thirty-foot wall—when the time came they lifted up a war cry and rushed into victory!

Desperate times call for desperate measures. Warrior, it is time to realize that these are desperate times. Where are the leaders who are willing to do whatever it takes to put their Savior first?

Complacency and compromise lull us to sleep, but desperation causes us to wake up.

> *"Awake, O sleeper, and arise from the dead, and Christ will shine on you."* ~ Ephesians 5:14

I believe, when this generation gets desperate for the presence of God, our condition will change from an *identity crisis* to a state of *revival*. Understand, revival doesn't happen because of a popular speaker or a big personality; it happens when God's people are corporately desperate for the Lord.

Just like Joshua, I urge you to awaken to God's presence.

Refuse to be silent.

Lead by example.

Let God stir a roar inside of your heart to break chains and release captives.

It is time to hear the WarCry of a prophet.

PART 2

WARCRY OF A PROPHET

[7]

ELIJAH'S CRY

You will leave no one, dead or alive, in the hands of the enemy.
~ U.S. Army Motto

CAN YOU IMAGINE HAVING a conversation with the prophet Elijah over a double-shot caramel macchiato from Starbucks?

I would ask the mighty prophet, "What was running through your mind when you stood up for God against 850 false prophets and fire fell from Heaven?"

I'd like to think Elijah would respond with something like this, "That's easy. I was thinking that you leave no one, dead or alive, in the hands of the enemy. I was afraid. I was outnumbered. I didn't have the perfect words, but I had a Word from the Lord."

1 Kings 18:36–37 records the mighty war cry that Elijah released over his generation from the top of Mount Carmel.

Full of faith, he stood in front of his enemy and cried out:

"LORD, the God of Abraham, Isaac and Israel, let it be known today that you are God in Israel and that I am your servant and have done all these things at your command. Answer me, LORD, answer me, so these

people will know that you, LORD, are God, and that you are turning their hearts back again."

Based on this cry, can you identify the word that Elijah heard from the Lord?

To turn the hearts of the people back to the one true God. This was the cry of Elijah as he stood on Mount Carmel against the idolatry of his generation.

Elijah took his stand: 450 prophets of Baal plus 400 prophets of Asherah against one prophet of Jehovah. Elijah didn't step up to battle with a superstar mentality. He stood as a response to God's call, "Turn their hearts back to me."

A true prophet is always called to turn the hearts of the people back to the one true God.

Tug of War

In Elijah's day, the people's hearts reflected the dry state of the land. For three and a half years, the land had no rain, and spiritually the people were just as dry. They were in a tug of war between worshipping God and worshipping Baal. In fact, the word "Baal" means "owner" or "master." The people of Israel were serving more than one master, and God was not pleased with their polluted worship. The Israelites were neither hot nor cold, but lukewarm, believing both Jehovah and Baal to be Lord. God was saying through the prophet Elijah, *"How long will you waver between two opinions? If the LORD is God, follow him; but if Baal is God, follow him"* (1 Kings 18:21).

Elijah, however, was not the first to speak for God.

The Israelites cried out in Exodus 2:23, so God raised up Moses to bust them out of Egypt. This was not the only time they would cry out for deliverance. God would later raise up Deborah, Samson, Elijah, Isaiah, Jeremiah, and countless others to stand in the gap. Every time a generation turned away from God and worshiped idols, the process would come full circle, and the people would cry out for a deliverer. **Then, God sent the ultimate warrior: *Jesus.*** Through His death and resurrection, Jesus gave you and I the authority to break spiritual chains.

When we offer pure worship to the Lord, untainted and desperate, the power that raised Jesus to life is released in a mighty way!

Elijah was unashamed to offer pure worship to the Lord, which is nothing to be taken lightly! In Elijah's generation, the prophets of Jehovah were being killed left and right. In fact, those who watched Elijah hike up Mount Carmel probably began preparing for his burial.

It would have been so easy for him to back down, but instead this man of God rose to the occasion. I'm so glad he did. Elijah's bold declaration broke chains off the people and ushered in an abundance of rain. Centuries later, we can still be a part of this powerful moment in time.

I encourage you to read through his story in 1 Kings 18 and put yourself on Mount Carmel next to Elijah as he released the WarCry of a prophet.

Ask yourself this question: *If I had been in Elijah's situation, would I have had the courage to speak up, or would I have been silent?*

You will answer this question every day as you encounter the idolatry in your generation.

IDOLS CANNOT SPEAK!

"Of what value is an idol carved by a craftsman? Or an image that teaches lies? For the one who makes it trusts in his own creation; he makes idols that cannot speak." ~ Habakkuk 2:18

In centuries past, people would choose a household "idol" based on the beauty given to it by its creator. It sounds silly to say that people would pray to a piece of wood or stone, but according to Habakkuk 2:19, that's exactly what they did.

They failed to realize that God never breathed into an idol and made it alive. Therefore, it cannot speak. Only humankind, created in God's image, can speak. Why do we take this for granted?

Instead of speaking for God, we turn away from Him and make idols for ourselves. Then we ask our own creation to speak for us. A piece of wood is not an idol any more than Facebook, money, or television is, but so often we carve our own idols from these meaningless elements. Even more dangerous is when a Christian creates an idol out of another Christian! When will we stop looking at pulpit ministry through the world's lens? There are no Christian celebrities, according to God! When a person preaches a powerful message, it breaks my heart to see the people of God applaud the vessel rather than the One who fills the vessel.

We have more in common with the Baal worshippers of Elijah's day than we realize. In fact, when I read about idolatry during that age, I see a mirror image of America. We have become so deceived that we can no longer tell the difference between male or female, life or death, true or false.

- The world says that any two people can be married if they love each other. God's word says, *That is why a* **man** *leaves his father and mother and is united to his* **wife**, *and they become one flesh* (Genesis 2:24).

- The world says that we hold the power to determine if an unborn child will live or die. God's word says, *"Before*

I formed you in the womb I knew you, before you were born I set you apart; I appointed you as a prophet to the nations" (Jeremiah 1:5b).

- The world says that strength comes from a strong physical stature, or a big personality. God's word says, *"My grace is sufficient for you, for my power is made perfect in weakness." Therefore I will boast all the more gladly about my weaknesses, so that Christ's power may rest on me* (2 Corinthians 12:9).

Idols are *not* a thing of the past; they are very active in our culture today. An idol is *anything* that we create and place above God.

Understand that the enemy is a copycat. He tries to mimic everything that God does in order to deceive us. Here is one example: *Your enemy the devil prowls around like a roaring lion looking for someone to devour* (1 Peter 5:8). This Scripture does not say the enemy is a lion, but rather he is *like* a lion, because he wants to scare the people of God into silence. The only true lion is Jesus Christ, who is the Lion of the Tribe of Judah! Do not be deceived by false images that simply try to reflect God's glory and take His fame.

Whether by parental examples or our own choices, many of us have created idols and false images for ourselves. The enemy then delights in using these meaningless objects to reflect an image of joy, peace, and love ... but they are only a mirror image! These idols and images only leave us feeling depressed and empty, because true joy is found in Jesus Christ. Eternal peace is found only at the foot of the cross. Lasting love entered the world through the death and resurrection of Jesus, not by the establishment of the Internet. Is Facebook your addiction? Get off Facebook and get on your face before God. Is the computer ruling your life? Stop allowing images that bring instant gratification to chain you up! The truth is we are all a reflection of something. What are you reflecting with your life?

We are God's creation and made in His image. Therefore, we speak. The enemy cannot be creative, speak life, or speak things into existence. Only God can, and because God can, we can! Stop letting false images lie to you. Take back your God-given ability to speak, and choose to leave no one, dead or alive, in the hands of the enemy. Idols clearly cannot speak! Child of the Most High God, only you were created to speak.

Carefully read through Ezekiel 24:27:

> "At that time your mouth will be opened; you will speak with him and will no longer be silent. So you will be a sign to them, and they will know that I am the LORD."

God's Word Never Fails

A fifth-century monk named Telemachus was led by a strong urgency to leave Asia and travel to Rome. This beautiful city was known for its creative architecture and bloody gladiator fights. Telemachus followed the crowds into the Coliseum, not knowing why the Spirit had led him there.

To everyone's surprise, the tiny monk jumped into the fighting ring and took a stand between two gladiators who were in the midst of a heated battle. At the top of his lungs, he cried out three times, "In the name of Christ, forbear!" Then, something happened that no one could have predicted. The angry crowds, who were so enraged by the interruption of their gladiator games, jumped to their feet and stoned

Telemachus to death.

Telemachus died that day as a martyr; however, his death was not in vain. Three days later, the Emperor decreed that the gladiator games would cease to exist. This fight went down in history as the last known gladiator fight in Rome and January 1, 404 A.D., was given the name Telemachus' Martyrdom.[6] This passionate little monk became a history-maker because he refused to be bullied into silence by the trends of his generation. He took a stand for the word that God had birthed in his spirit, and he released a cry that shook the entire country of Rome.

The Bible recounts a number of individuals, young and old, male and female, from all nationalities, that took a stand for God.

Shadrach, Meshach, and Abednego took a stand and saw a miracle in the fiery furnace. Deborah took a stand and led an outnumbered army into victory over an impossible enemy. David took a stand and killed a giant with a slingshot. Joshua took a stand and saw the walls of a grand city come tumbling down. Paul and Silas took a stand and witnessed an earthquake that broke chains. The disciples took a stand and witnessed healings, miracles, and breakthroughs, time and time again.

This list could go on for miles! If I were to add your name to this list, what would it say about you?

Of course, we cannot forget about Elijah the prophet, who took a bold and unashamed stand on Mount Carmel. Thus ensued one of the most dramatic presentations of good versus evil the world has ever known.

Atop Mount Carmel, I believe onlookers could see the showdown taking place as if it were screened worldwide from

Hollywood. After the prophets of Baal had ceased their pagan worship, it was Elijah's turn to step up to the plate. He repaired the altar that had been torn down by the Baal worshippers and replaced it with an altar of pure worship to Jehovah.

Then, Elijah turned his eyes to the sky and lifted his voice. He declared the words of God and a demonstration of Jehovah's power followed as fire fell from Heaven. Demonstrations of God's power should follow our WarCry because the Kingdom of Heaven is one of both declaration *and* demonstration. That day, the prophets of Baal were defeated and the people of God were set free. Rain finally returned to the land.

You see, God's word *never fails*. The reason why Telemachus and Elijah took a stand centuries ago, and the reason why we can stand today is because God's word never fails. It is the same yesterday, today, and forever. God's word never comes up short and never returns void (Isaiah 55:11, KJV). Because God's word never fails, we can be confident when we speak His word.

In 2013, we found ourselves smack in the middle of one of the driest areas of Texas. There was nothing but parched land and open fields for miles. This was the backdrop for the youth camp we had been invited to speak at.

Come to find out, this area of Texas had been in severe drought for an entire year. Coming from Florida, this was a unique situation for our team.

Worship started the first night, and the presence of God filled the open-air pavilion. I will never forget worshiping toward the left upper corner of the pavilion. Staring out at the beautiful landscape, I felt the Holy Spirit speak to my heart, "Get ready; the rain is coming!" My mind ran immediately to the third night, which was to be focused on the Holy

Spirit. I thought, "Awesome, Lord! You are going to send an outpouring of your Spirit!"

However, God was about to blow my mind yet again.

As the third day of camp began, games commenced as usual. The only difference was a slight breeze in the air. Around noon, dark clouds swept in out of nowhere. Within a short time, the heavens opened and rain clouds let loose. It didn't just rain it *poured*.

The scene was priceless as leaders were frantically trying to shove students under the pavilion, into the lunchroom, dorms, or anywhere thy could find. Imagine students dancing in the rain like little kids on Christmas morning. These Texans were so in awe of something that I take for granted every single day. Florida summers are no stranger to rainstorms, but these students were rejoicing in the beauty of a pure rainfall, despite the lightning and strong winds that accompanied it.

That night, God also poured out His Holy Spirit in a powerful way! Sons and daughters were filled with the Spirit as they pressed into the presence of God late into the night.

I believe this reflects the state of our nation. Right now, America is wandering in a desert place. There are countless people who are hungry, in extreme poverty, addicted to drugs, and suffering abuse. Where should these people turn—the Church, right?

Unfortunately, the Church is sick and in desperate need of revival. The "get famous quick" mentality has swept across America, affecting many believers in its path. It seems like written materials are in abundance, but that the word of the Lord is actually quite rare. Christians have resource after resource available at their fingertips, yet walk in very little power and authority. Too often we are found with a declaration, but no sincere demonstration.

Our world is dead and dry, limping between multiple opinions as the Israelites were. But we must not neglect the fact that God is doing something new. I urge you not to give up on the Church of Jesus Christ. We need you to fight for her. We need you to love her as the generations have done. My heart longs for an outpouring of the Spirit that invades every area of our world—similar to the New Testament Church, but more widespread.

Elijah spoke God's word and healing returned to the land. In the same way, your words create pathways in the wilderness and rivers in the desert. When the Holy Spirit is within you and you begin to speak the promises of God over your generation, you become like a river in a dry place.

[8]

BORN TO ROAR

*"I am not afraid of an army of lions led by a sheep;
I am afraid of an army of sheep led by a lion."*
~ Alexander the Great

HUNDREDS OF STUDENTS FLOODED into the gym with the sole purpose of seeking God's face during their weekly youth service. I was in the corner with my face down when God said to me, "Look up; what do you see?"

I gazed up at the vast group of students. Some were pacing back in forth with the passion of a preacher, tearing down spiritual strongholds with the fire of God. Others were kneeling and pleading for God's outpouring on their generation. The corners were packed with even more students worshipping with their hands raised and hearts ablaze.

"God, I see students seeking Your face."

God responded, "I see an army."

The Holy Spirit reminded me of Ezekiel 37:9–10 (AMP):

Then He said to me, "Prophesy to the breath, son of man, and say to the breath, 'Thus says the Lord God: "Come from the four winds, O breath, and breathe on these slain, that they may live."" So I prophesied as He commanded me, and the breath came into them, and they lived and stood on their feet, an exceedingly great army.

In this Scripture, God provided specific instructions: *Prophesy to the breath.* Ezekiel simply obeyed, and an army was resurrected back to life.

Harnessing the power of your words and releasing them at the *God-appointed time* will usher in a move of the Holy Spirit that will transcend human limitation.

Prophecy Broken Down

I know that the word "prophesy" can sound intimidating, but don't let it intimidate you! To prophesy is basically to "speak" out God's divine Word at a divinely-appointed moment in time.

Even though Old Testament prophecy was often intended to predict the future, prophecy is not primarily about foretelling. Rather, it is about forth-telling, or declaring that which cannot be known by natural means (Matthew 26:68), and is the revelation of the will of God with reference to the past, present, or future (Genesis 20:7, Revelation 10:11).

God has clearly appointed specific people to the office of prophet throughout the generations, but this does not exclude all other believers from functioning in the prophetic. In fact, there is a prophetic call on the life of every believer!

Check this out:

> *"'In the last days, God says, I will pour out my Spirit on ALL people. Your sons and daughters will prophesy, your young men will see visions, your old men will dream dreams. Even on my servants, both men and women, I will pour out my Spirit in those days, and they will prophesy.'"* ~ Acts 2:17–18

As long as they are consecrated to God, all of His children have the Holy Spirit dwelling inside of them; therefore, prophecy can come from any believer, anywhere, at any time! *Do not over-complicate your understanding of prophecy and do not diminish its power!*

In small groups, we enter into the Scriptures, each exploring and applying God's word to our own situations. This gives every believer the opportunity to prophesy.

During evangelistic outreach, we share the message of Jesus with unbelievers. This also gives every believer the opportunity to prophesy.

I believe that the spirit of prophecy needs to return to every believer within the church, because the Holy Spirit dwells within all believers. While not everyone is called to prophesy on stage during a worship service, everyone is called to speak to the "dry bones" in their world. Status, title, and position do not determine an individual's ability to function in the prophetic, because it is only through intimacy with the Lord that prophetic insight is birthed.

Jesus told the disciples that when they receive the Holy Spirit, they would become His witnesses (Acts 1:8). The word *witnesses* here is actually the root of the same word for *testimony* found in Revelation 19:10.

This means that you and I are witnesses so that we may testify to the Gospel—the spirit of prophecy is the testimony of Jesus! Prophecy is completely Gospel-focused and, therefore, we are witnesses as we prophesy to our lost world about Jesus Christ.

Let us heed the call to boldly declare the Gospel. I strongly believe that God is looking for surrendered vessels like Ezekiel, who will step up to the valley of dry bones in their generation and proclaim the word of the Lord.

The WarCry of a Prophet: Alexis

Alexis was the president of the Christian club at her high school. Over the course of the year, the club had grown from 10 to over 150 students in weekly attendance. All year, she continued to lead this army of students in prayer and outreach on her campus. Alexis was a warrior who was unafraid to prophesy to the empty, dry, dead places of her public high school.

A few weeks prior to graduation, the unexpected death of a classmate rattled the students at UHS. Alexis decided that this suicide would not be the final event of the 2014 school year. Led by the Spirit, Alexis called the entire school to a time of prayer during their lunch hour. Over 1,000 students poured out of the lunchroom and headed toward the courtyard to pray.

Despite an attack of silence, Alexis refused to be silent. Alexis made history that day as she led almost the entire student body in prayer. Here's the awesome part: Alexis did not just pray that day; she went to battle. Alexis prophesied in the same way that Ezekiel did when he spoke to the valley of dry bones. God gave her a word, and she boldly called dead places to come to life, chains to be broken, and hurting people to be restored. She declared idols to be broken off her school in the name of Jesus and that people would return to the Lord. When everyone else was silent and defeated, Alexis released a WarCry that broke the chains of suicide off her campus.

Alexis was a history-maker. Not because she was the prom queen, even though she was. And not because she was the president of the campus club, even though she was. Alexis was a history-maker because she made a bold declaration that God was number one in her life and needed to be number one in her world. That year, Alexis's WarCry left an unforgettable mark on her high school.

As we prophesy, or speak, to the dead places of our world in obedience to God, chains will break and lives will be returned to the one true God.

At the beginning of the 2014 school year, Pen Florida Youth Alive recorded a video of Alexis's outcry for her campus. This is what she said at the beginning of her senior year: "A few weeks ago God gave me a vision and I saw all the students in the school worshipping in the courtyard."

This was the vision that Alex carried in her heart the entire school year. A few weeks prior to her senior graduation, this dream came to pass. Now, death and depression are no longer the chains that UHS will remember when they think of the 2014 class. Instead, they will remember the bold warrior who stood up in the face of darkness and released the WarCry of a prophet.

There's an Army Rising Up

Throughout Scripture, there is a second Hebrew word that means war cry.

That word is *tsarach*, meaning *to cry* or *to release a roar*.

The Lord spoke to my heart that the WarCry of a prophet is to release a roar that casts aside deeds of darkness and breaks chains!

I wish I could fully describe to you the roar that the word *tsarach* refers to, but it is almost indescribable until you have experienced it for yourself. In all honesty, I do not think any person will experience this roar fully until we all enter into

Heaven. We can, however, understand that a roar is not a one-time noise that comes from your throat. It is, rather, a cry from the depths of your soul, a cry that cannot be held back, a cry that must be released!

As your WarCry is released, you dig deeper into the presence of God. This mighty cry declares that God reigns above all others and is the only one worthy to be praised. When you are equipped with the WarCry of a prophet, you put on prophetic ammunition that strikes fear into the enemy and raises up prophetic worship.

There is power in just one passionate chain-breaker like Alexis, but imagine the day when a multitude of believers will rise up with the same passion and purpose. Chains will fall off from every corner of our world!

One of my favorite songs by Hillsong declares, *There's an army rising up, to break every chain*. I believe that God is calling a massive army, equipped with prophetic ammunition and consecrated hearts, to arise from the ashes of their pasts for the purpose of breaking chains.

Revelation 19:6 (ESV) illustrates this magnificent army that God is raising up in the last days to break chains:

> *Then I heard what seemed to be the voice of a great multitude, like the roar of many waters and like the sound of mighty peals of thunder, crying out, "Hallelujah! For the Lord our God the Almighty reigns."*

The book of Revelation is one of the most unique books in all of Scripture, as it deals with predictive prophecy. We can determine from Revelation 19 that the apostle John clearly sees a massive army that roars as one voice with one mission. This vision is actually a prediction of what is to come.

The war cry of the army of God in Revelation 19 is so mighty that it echoes like that of water crashing down Niagara Falls or thunder booming across the skies. Without a doubt, this roar vibrates throughout the heavens. It is the Lord's army, resounding a mighty war cry over and over again: *"Hallelujah! For the Lord our God the Almighty reigns!"* (Revelation 19:6b, ESV).

Warrior, you were born to roar.

NOT ALL CATS ROAR

Only four cats can roar: the lion, tiger, leopard, and jaguar. A lion or tiger can roar as loud as 114 decibels, which is about 25 times louder than a gas-powered lawn mower! However, not all cats roar, because not all cats were created to roar. Not all cats have the special rectangle-shaped vocal fold that allows them to release a roar. This simple, yet profound characteristic identifies these cats that roar as the genus *Panthera*.

The same is true for Christians. They were all *created* to roar but they all don't *choose* to roar.

All believers have an innate ability to prophesy, or speak God word to their generation, even if only to their next-door neighbor. All believers are empowered by the Holy Spirit to release a bold word and testify about Jesus. Every Christian has the ability to worship at a deeper level and unleash a word that sends the enemy fleeing. All believers are born to roar. However, many are bound by fear and complacency. They prefer to sit back and allow others to do the roaring, but the time has come for all believers to step up and release the WarCry of a prophet! We need you to realize who you were created to be and release a roar that shakes the world around you.

Your height, size, voice, and limitations do not determine your roar. In a study of animals that roar, it was discovered that neither the size of the animal nor the size of the vocal fold determined its ability or strength to roar.

This excites me, because I am 4'11 ¾". Let me tell you, this little body is unashamed and unafraid to release a roar. I have seen the atmosphere of a room of 400 students change because one unseen individual released a roar in worship. This sparked a chain reaction, which sent the entire room into breakthrough worship. Nothing physical determines the strength of your roar; it is all based on your intimacy with God.

Breakthrough Worship

In war times past, soldiers were often commanded to release their war cry through song as they approached the battle line.

Why, you may ask?

The battle strategy was simple: psych out the enemy.

Strong soldiers know if they can strike fear into the opposing army, cowardice will cause the enemy to flee before the fight has even begun. It is proven that even a stronger enemy will be discouraged by a weaker team crashing shields and swords against one another, blasting trumpets, and roaring loudly.

In the same way, spiritual battles must be fought with spiritual weapons. As we release a WarCry in worship, we psych out the enemy; he has no idea what to do, so he flees! The enemy cannot handle a unified roar from the children of God. This breakthrough worship ushers in a roar that will shake the very doorposts of your room.

Are you afraid? Worship. Do you feel alone? Worship. Are you faced with an overwhelming situation? Worship. I believe that this is exactly what happened when Paul and Silas worshiped God from inside their jail cell. A roar was released, the foundations of the cell shook, and chains broke off!

A roar is powerful because it raises a cloud of God's presence that surrounds worshipers like smoke from a mighty wildfire. When a lion roars, it can be heard as far away as five miles and have enough force to raise a cloud of dust.

In his vision, John noticed that, the more God was worshiped, the more smoke arose from the "prostitute," which is a symbol for sin (Revelation 19:3). The louder and longer this mighty army raised a WarCry, the more smoke arose from the sin! Don't forget: our Champion has already won the battle. But as worship goes up from the people of God, bondages break and chains fall off. Just as a lion's roar can create a cloud of dust, your roar creates a cloud of God's presence!

God searches the world for those who will worship Him in spirit and in truth (John 4:24), because His army is not composed of singers, but worshipers. I believe that God looked down from Heaven and could not take His eyes off of Paul and Silas when they were in that jail cell. Not because they could sing well or harmonize together, but because they were worshiping God in the midst of an impossible situation, proving they were true worshipers.

Trust me, you do not want me to lead a song, but I can still lead worship. I am not a singer, but I am a worshiper. A true worshiper can lead in worship from any corner of the room, not just on the stage. A common misassumption is that it is solely the responsibility of the worship team to usher in the presence of God. I believe that, as true worshipers get corporately desperate for God, they will release a roar that ushers in the Spirit of God in powerful ways. I believe there will be a day when revival will start not with a speaker or a worship team, but with the people of God simply becoming hungry for more of God.

The army that God is raising up will convict sinners with the power of their words, because they are clothed with consecrated hearts. The weapons of this army do not consist of arrows, swords, or bomb—but a roar.

[9]

CHAIN-BREAKER, HISTORY-MAKER

*"To forgive is to set a prisoner free
and discover that the prisoner was you."*
~ Lewis B. Smedes

*Don't allow the new thing that God is doing to be hindered
by the old thing that once held you captive. It is time to let go!*

IN THE HEAT OF World War II, Corporal Jacob DeShazer successfully completed his mission when he airdropped a bomb onto an opposing Japanese city. However, lack of fuel and no place to land left this soldier with only two options: crash and die, or eject and be captured by the enemy.

Choosing the best option for survival, DeShazer ejected from the plane. He was captured and confined in a Japanese prison camp for almost two years. Sickness, exhaustion, and starvation all threatened to take his life, but God had a different plan for this lonely and forgotten soldier.

DeShazer and the other prisoners were allowed to read

during their confinement. DeShazer waited six months before finally getting his hands on the Bible, a luxury that many Americans take for granted!

Romans 10:9 stood out to this prisoner of war, and on the spot he surrendered to God on the spot. God began giving DeShazer a passion for reaching his enemies with the Gospel of Jesus Christ. He quickly became friends with his captors, leading some of them to the Lord. God had truly worked a miracle in his life, but the story doesn't end there.

A year after his salvation experience, the prisoners were transferred to Beijing. One morning, DeShazer awoke at 7:00 feeling to pray for peace. Tired and confused, he dropped to his knees and began to pray.

As 2:00 in the afternoon rolled around, the Lord spoke to his heart again, "You don't need to pray any longer. The victory is won!"

What this prisoner of war did not know was that atomic bomb had just been released on Hiroshima. We now know August 6, 1945, as a day that America took a stand for freedom.

The American soldiers quickly released DeShazer and the others from Japanese captivity. To his surprise, he was the only freed prisoner who was not rejoicing. Quite the opposite! He was deeply saddened by the pain of the Japanese in the wake of the bombing. He was concerned for those who had held him captive.

This burden continued to grow, and, in 1948, the Lord called him to return to Japan as a missionary. Upon returning, this soldier-turned-missionary was shocked to hear that army chaplains had already passed out over a million tracts containing his testimony. The tracks we entitled, *I Was a Prisoner of the Japanese*.[7]

To his surprise, the entire country wanted to hear the story of the soldier who was able to forgive his captors!

Eventually, his ultimate dream was fulfilled when he planted a church in the same city he had bombed right before being captured.

DeShazer's story is one of love and forgiveness. God used this prisoner of war to help break chains off the Japanese nation, but first he had to release his own chains of unforgiveness. After this army corporal became a chain-breaker, his story became legendary and he was forever known as a history-maker.

Spiritual chains bind up those who do not forgive. God's victory through DeShazer would not have been possible had he not forgiven the captors who had brutally tortured him for years.

From Slavery to Adoption

For many years, I lived under the chain of unforgiveness. I was angry at my mom, with my dad, and even myself. This blocked the overflow of God's love in my life and threatened to silence me. In fact, I lived for a long time under the false notion that I was an orphan. Not because I did not have parents, but I felt like a spiritual orphan.

The number of actual orphans throughout the world is devastating, but the amount of teenagers who live with one or both parents, yet still feel spiritually orphaned, is shocking as well.

Loneliness seemed to mark every stage of my childhood, but here is the real clincher: even after surrendering my life to the Lord, I continued to live as though I was a spiritual orphan.

I think that explains some of my connection to the Disney character named Peter Pan. I can relate to him because he could fly, which I think is awesome.

Many fail to remember that Peter Pan actually chose to be an orphan. While each of the Lost Boys entered into the Darling family and received a new last name, Peter Pan refused to open his heart. He chose a life of solitude rather than a life of love.

Many individuals find themselves in this exact same situation. The orphan spirit on this generation has left many—even some with actual parents—living under the lie that they are spiritual orphans, looking for love, acceptance, and guidance in all the wrong places. God has His arms wide open, but we must choose to enter into His family.

One day, God brought a realization to my heart. He said, "You do not know your identity in me and, therefore, you have been silent. I have adopted you and I am telling you now, don't ever let anyone bully you into silence ever again." I was silenced to the chain-breaking authority that God had for me because I did not understand my adoption.

Christ died so that you could receive the Holy Spirit and be adopted as a child of God. Realize your identity in Christ, and you will realize your chain-breaking potential.

> *For all who are led by the Spirit of God are sons [children] of God. For you did not receive the spirit of slavery to fall back into fear, but you have received the Spirit of adoption.* ~ Romans 8:14-15a, ESV

Wow! Understanding your adoption breaks off a spirit of slavery and empowers you through the Holy Spirit to break chains. This is a powerful reminder that when we give our lives to the Lord and fling aside every snare of sin, we are no longer a slave bound up by spiritual chains. We are the adopted children of God! Our identity is no longer that of a slave, but that of an heir.

Do you see? *Adoption = Empowerment.*

Before you can break chains, you must understand that you are no longer under a spirit of slavery, but a spirit of adoption—the Holy Spirit, to be exact!

This empowerment of the Holy Spirit transitions the average, ordinary believer into an extraordinary warrior for the Kingdom of God. And in order to release the WarCry of a prophet over our generation, we must first release the chains that hold us back from knowing our identity in Christ.

As an adopted child, you inherit a position for when you arrive in Heaven, but also for this life as well. Just as He healed me, God wants to restore to you the years that the enemy has stolen and give you an inheritance that flows from heavenly places.

Only by deeply understanding my adoption in Christ did I finally come to the point where I could forgive my mother and father. God takes forgiveness very seriously, because if we do not forgive others of their sins, the Father will not forgive us of our sins (Matthew 6:15). If the Lord can forgive us, then in His strength we can forgive each other. Decide right now that you will not allow the chain of unforgiveness to keep you from reaching your fullest potential in Christ.

DEAL WITH DEEDS OF DARKNESS

"The night is nearly over; the day is almost here. So let us put aside the deeds of darkness..." ~ Romans 13:12

Spiritual chains, such as unforgiveness and others listed in

1 Timothy 3, are the result of deeds of darkness that hold us captive to our own desires.

As Kingdom warriors, we must do as Romans 13:12 says and "put aside" (*cast off, throw away,* or *fling off*) those deeds of darkness that seek to hold us captive. These chains have no place in our lives or in our generation.

That's why 2 Corinthians 10:3–6 is a powerful Scripture that urges us to take every thought captive that "exalts itself," or *seeks praise,* over the knowledge of God.

We must learn to take our thoughts captive, or our thoughts will take us captive! Any area of our lives bound up by religion, sin, bad habits, or wrong thought patterns is a place of stronghold. This is one way the enemy seeks to silence us, but there is power in the name of Jesus to break every chain!

In the Name of Jesus

Paul and Silas understood that there is power in the name of Jesus. In Acts 16, Paul spoke the name of Jesus and a girl was immediately set free from chains of divination.

> *Then Paul, being greatly annoyed and worn out, turned and said to the spirit [inside her], "I command you in the name of Jesus Christ [as His representative to come out of her!" And it came out that very moment.*
> ~ Acts 16:18, AMP

The power of the enemy is no match for the power that resides in the name of Jesus! However, the next thing Paul and Silas knew, they were being tortured and sent to prison for this "act of treason." They were taken as prisoners of war, thrown into a maximum-security cell, and chained up with leg irons (Acts 16:24).

As midnight approached Paul and Silas were praying

and singing a *robust hymn to God* (Acts 16:25b, MSG). There is a strong chance that these disciples had been worshiping for hours when the clock finally struck midnight. I can imagine the war cry that begins to stir in their spirits as they worshiped God in the midst of their chains. It probably wasn't the gorgeous harmony of a worship team like in our day, but it was oozing with the power of the cross.

Their powerful praise produced an incredible earthquake that shook the very foundations of the prison. The Bible records so vividly that all the prison doors were shaken open and every prisoner was loosed! Even the captors were so taken aback by the power of God that they surrendered their lives to Jesus. The breaking of physical chains brought about the demolishing of spiritual chains.

Just like Corporal Jacob DeShazer, Paul and Silas were prisoners of war.

Records show that by the completion of World War II, there were thousands of American prisoners of war all over Asia, Europe, and Africa.

However, this number fails in comparison to the number of spiritual prisoners of war—men and women who carry heavy chains that keep them bound to unforgiveness and an unfulfilled life.

Are you a prisoner of war? Hear me clearly today: there is power in the name of Jesus to break every chain!

The Holy Spirit penetrated DeShazer's cell of darkness and broke every chain off his life, both spiritually and physically. God wants to do the same thing for you.

Jesus, the light of the world, wants to radiate light into the dark places so that chains can be broken and people can be set free. Do you realize the power that exists simply by speaking the name of Jesus over your situation?

God has bestowed on Christ the name that is above every name, and at this name every knee must bow and every tongue confess that Jesus is Lord (Philippians 2:9–11). We are even told to pray "in the name of Jesus," because His name is powerful (John 14:13). Don't misunderstand this verse. The name of Jesus is not a magic formula that will result in all of your wishes being granted. On the contrary, it holds power to demolish strongholds and break chains! Praying "in the name of Jesus" is coming into agreement with God's will.

The name of Jesus is the only thing that will set the captive free and release the prisoners of war in our generation.

The precious blood of Jesus was shed in the cruelest way possible so that chains could be broken. From this blood flows freedom; we simply have to receive it. By receiving the blood of Jesus, we receive adoption into the Kingdom of God. That is why the name of Jesus breaks chains when spoken from the mouth of one who is adopted. The blood of Jesus and the word inside of us are like ammunition, but we must open our mouths and speak!

I have witnessed countless people who are afraid to step up and share their testimony with just one person, let alone a group of people. This breaks my heart, because it is an attack of the enemy to silence the people of God. Evil is pushed back when we testify (Revelation 12:11). We must learn to declare what God has done, because our words are powerful.

For this reason, the WarCry of a prophet serves to release a roar that breaks chains off your generation.

The power to break chains is not in the WarCry itself, but rather comes straight from God, who is our ultimate warrior. The WarCry is a tool, or a way of communicating the will of God on Earth. We are simply the vessel, but when we are in alignment with His heart, we can function in Christ's authority.

Warrior, you are the light of the world. You must trudge into the dark prison cells and release prisoners of war. You must carry the sword of the Spirit into places of brokenness. You are a chain-breaker, because the power of God dwells inside of you. Now, walk in freedom and release a roar over your generation.

If you, or someone you know, needs to walk in total freedom, begin by praying this prayer, but don't just pray; enter into spiritual battle.

Father God, thank you for sending Your son Jesus to die for my sins. I am sorry for sinning and I ask You to forgive me. Thank You for adopting me into Your family and loving me even when I was lost. I pray for the blood of Jesus right now to be released over my mind so that I may walk in victory. I also declare that in the Name of Jesus that the chain of _____ will be broken off of my life. Thank you. In the matchless name of Jesus, amen.

PART 3

WARCRY OF A KING

[10]

The Armor of Light

"Don't let anyone bully you into silence."
~ Harvey Fierstein

WHAT AM I HERE *for? What am I not doing that I am supposed to be doing?* Night after night, these overwhelming questions consumed my mind. As I lay in the darkness of my bedroom, I could not shake the voice in my heart saying, *There is something important I want you to do.*

One night I became so fed up with these endless inquiries that I sat completely upright in bed and shouted, "What, God?! What am I not doing that I need to be doing?" I felt exhilarated when I finally identified where the voice was coming from: *God.* In that moment, an explosion of even more questions ran through my mind.

How could God be speaking to me? Does God even speak to people? Years of Catholic masses ran through my mind.

Yes, God spoke to people in Bible times, but how could the Creator of the universe be speaking to me now? I am not Moses. I am not Mary. I am certainly not King David. I closed my eyes and fought to get back to sleep. Certainly, God was not speaking to me. And yet, deep down, I knew that God was calling me to go higher.

The problem was not that I didn't want to respond to God, nor was it that I was afraid. It was simply the fact that I was not equipped. I was not empowered. The Holy Spirit was calling me into a deeper relationship with God, but I did not understand this calling.

There are countless people in this world who have felt the leading of the Holy Spirit, but are unequipped and unempowered to take deeper steps in their relationship with Christ. The Church as a whole needs a stronger understanding of the person of the Holy Spirit and His empowerment in the life of every believer.

No one entered my bedroom and told me to respond to the voice of God. It was the Spirit calling me deeper. You and I do not equip or empower people; this is solely the work of the Holy Spirit. We are instruments that the Lord carefully and beautifully plays in order to draw other people closer to Him.

A few weeks after the questions began, God answered me in a way I did not expect.

One afternoon, my dad was driving me home from school. As we passed St. Stephen's Catholic Church, the Holy Spirit whispered to my heart, *This is what you are going to do for the rest of your life.*

I had grown up in this church, with its tall peaks reaching to the sky and its pristine grass baking under the Florida sun. In that moment, it was a perfect example of grace and poise. We called it our "home church," which meant we attended on Christmas and Easter.

The first thought that entered my young mind was, *God,*

I'm sorry, but I absolutely, positively refuse to be a nun!

Thankfully, the Lord had a better plan than what I could comprehend at the time.

Looking back, this was the day that God officially called me into ministry, but it was not until many years later that I finally became ordained with the Assemblies of God denomination. Now you can understand the relief and amazement that I felt when I walked into a Pentecostal youth service for the first time and discovered I could serve in ministry without being a nun.

When my husband and I became Youth Alive missionaries for the state of Florida, it was this gripping pain—the need to understand our purpose in life—that led us to launch this ministry of building students who are equipped for service and empowered for battle. The truth is, no matter where you work, attend school, or go grocery shopping, there are people everywhere who are looking for answers to these plaguing questions: *Why am I here? What is my purpose?* You have the privilege of helping them answer these questions. You, my friend, are a light in the darkness, sent out by God as a warrior on a mission to lead others to Christ.

The word "mission" is in "missionary" for a reason! None of us are truly home while we are on this Earth; we are missionaries. While there is still breath in your lungs, you are not on vacation but on mission.

Missing In Action

Following World War II, the U.S. Armed Forces recorded 78,750 soldiers as "missing in action" (MIA). Essentially, out of the number of soldiers that had been killed, at least 20% were simply "lost" in war as a result of death, captivity, or being deserted by fellow soldiers.

In today's society, it is clear that many Christians are MIA. They are saved and headed to Heaven, but are not showing up to battle. Not only that, but many who do show up do not understand the spiritual armor that is to be worn by believers.

Ephesians 6:14 paints a clear picture of the spiritual armor that is to be worn when we engage in warfare:

> Belt of truth buckled around your waist.
>
> The breastplate of righteousness in place.
>
> Feet fitted with the readiness that comes from the gospel of peace.
>
> The shield of faith.
>
> Take the helmet of salvation.
>
> The sword of the Spirit, which is the word of God.
>
> Pray in the Spirit on all occasions.

No warrior or knight would dream of entering a battle without his or her suit of armor. Why should spiritual soldiers be any different? Spiritual armor is either a foreign concept or completely neglected by many Christians. Look at our world! Believers are not stepping up to do their part, and the ones that are become quickly burned out or quit. Where are all the Christians? Sadly, they are missing in action.

Warrior, the Holy Spirit wants to equip you with spiritual armor so that you can be prepared for battle, rather than retreat in fear.

Historical armor served two primary purposes: to save the life of the soldier, and to function as a status symbol.[8]

At first, a soldier's armor was very stiff and weak, but it was strengthened over time as it became fitted to the soldier's body. The process of putting on armor was no joke, either. Just as a football player needs his pads, a knight required special plate armor for survival. Many historians believe that this process took almost thirty minutes.

In the same way, it often takes a Christian time and preparation to suit up for battle. One does not don the shield of faith without going through experiences that require faith, or effectively wield the sword of truth until they have pondered the power of Scripture.

Learning to wear spiritual armor is a process that takes time and spiritual strength, which is very similar to the war heroes of old. However, the difference between your armor and theirs is that spiritual armor radiates from within as pure light. This glow is the glory of God shining off of His warriors, as we minister from under the anointing. This is what makes our armor different from that of the world—it is the armor of light!

1. Put on the Armor of Light

So then let us cast off the works of darkness and put on the armor of light. ~ Romans 13:12b, ESV, emphasis added

Here's the catch: God does not just force us into armor the moment we are saved. On the contrary, we must first *cast off* works of darkness and then *put on* the armor of light.

In Exodus 34, Moses had spent a considerable amount of time with God on Mount Sinai, receiving the Ten Commandments. Then, as he descended the mountain and stepped into the Israelite camp, the people could actually see the glory of God shining off of Moses's face. It was so bright that the people were afraid to speak to him. Moses was wearing the armor of light, and everyone in the Israelite camp noticed.

Scripture reveals the same thing in the New Testament: God's glory radiated in the darkness through Jesus Christ. Even though it was not visible on Jesus' skin, the disciples were lucky enough one night to see through a spiritual window into the divine image of Jesus: *There he was transfigured before them. His face shone like the sun, and his clothes became as white as the light* (Matthew 17:2). Jesus radiated light so strongly that everywhere He went people were saved, healed, and delivered.

Today, the anointing is revealed through the third person of the Trinity—the Holy Spirit. When the Spirit of God descended for the first time at Pentecost, the infilling became visible through tongues of fire. Believers no longer had to dwell in a temple, or spend countless hours in religious practices. The presence of God began to dwell inside of them as an internal flame, because the believer actually became the temple. The power of God radiated so strongly from the early Church pioneers that even their own shadows brought about healing.

The presence of God dwells in us in the same way today. When we spend time in prayer and worship, the Holy Spirit clothes us with the armor of light and power from on high. As we function in the unique calling that God has prepared for us, an anointing is released and the light of the Lord radiates through the darkness in a powerful way!

For this reason, trying to spread the Gospel without wearing the armor of light is like Katniss Everdeen trying to win the Hunger Games without her bow and arrow. To fight spiritual battles that transcend our world, we must be equipped with armor that is not of this world, but rather is of divine design.

It is absolutely necessary that we spend time in the presence of God so that we can put on the armor of light. Just like Moses, who spent countless hours with the Lord, we too must prioritize our time with God in order to be clothed in the armor of light.

2. Refuse to Wear Another's Armor

Then Saul outfitted David as a soldier in armor. He put his bronze helmet on his head and belted his sword on him over the armor. David tried to walk but he could hardly budge. David told Saul, "I can't even move with all this stuff on me. I'm not used to this." And he took it all off. ~ 1 Samuel 17:38–39, MSG

History books record that armor had to be tailor-made for soldiers entering battle, because it was imperative that the armor fits as well as possible. In the same way, God has tailor-made our armor to fit our specific calling.

Can you imagine if the president of the United States took off his suit jacket and placed it on your shoulders prior to you arriving at school or work? What an honor! You would probably strut around school with serious bragging rights.

This may have been the way David felt prior to his battle with Goliath. To wear the armor of your king into battle was one of the highest honors a soldier could receive. All of David's big brothers stood speechless as they witnessed their youngest brother receive the king's armor in 1 Samuel.

David, however, was not concerned with an earthly audience, as only a divine audience captivated his heart. To everyone's surprise, he refused to enter into battle against Goliath wearing the armor of another soldier—even if that person was the king of Israel.

David had spent so much time in God's presence that he was sensitive to the leading of the Holy Spirit. He knew that Saul's armor was not fitting for him or his calling. So, he shrugged off Saul's armor and set out to find his own—a stone and a sling, accompanied by his shepherd's staff and bag.

As I grew in my relationship with the Lord, there were many times I attempted to wear the armor of another soldier, but I can't name a single time when it was successful. A powerful speaker would share at my youth group, and the following week I would attempt to speak in the same manner as that person. Sometimes we become so caught up in the glitz and glamour of Christian "celebrities" that we start to desire their spiritual armor. We think, *If I just sing like this, act like that, or preach this way, then I will be successful.* This is a trap of the enemy. God has not called you to someone else's mission, so why would He want you to wear their armor?

Never wear the armor of another soldier!

Instead, spend time with the Lord and ask Him to reveal to you the calling and purpose that He has for your life. The Holy Spirit wants to equip and empower you with armor, weapons, and a mission tailor-made to you.

3. Stand Your Ground

> *Therefore, put on the complete armor of God, so that you will be able to [successfully] resist and stand your ground in the evil day [of danger], and having done everything [that the crisis demands], to stand firm*

[in your place, fully prepared, immovable, victorious]. ~ Ephesians 6:13, AMP

The Lord empowers us by His Spirit to wear the armor of God, but you must put it on so you can stand your ground. It is only in God's strength that you are unshakable.

As a young person, I constantly felt pressure to perform and pursue a destiny that was not meant for me. It seemed as though my dad tried everything he could to make me independent, but in doing so, he also taught me how to put up walls. Sadly, my father lived in so much bondage himself that he could not see the pain he was causing me. Eventually, I began to turn *his* bondage into *my* bondage. A legacy of silence continued in our family, until I finally decided it was time for a change.

The Lord broke the generational curse of silence off my life when I decided that other people did not have the power to define me. I finally traded in my old labels for my destiny when I married a minister, graduated from Bible college, and became a minister myself. I slowly began to clothe myself with the armor of light. I wish I could tell you this transformation was instantaneous, but it took years. Spiritually, I was set free when I gave my life to Jesus, but I continued to physically live as if I was still in bondage. Flesh is slow to action and requires discipline.

During this season of preparation, and even now, there are times when I feel overwhelmed, weary, and defeated ... but through it all I chose to never give up and turn my back on the Lord. I realized that, in the midst of struggle, sometimes all I can do is stand. When you have given everything you can, the time comes to dig your feet into the dirt and take a stand on the promises of God—in the midst of the storm and pain, stand on the word of God and His truth.

Even if it took all I had, I was going to stand. While fear and fleeing used to be my gut reactions to difficulty, I now declare that turning back is never an option.

I realized that I shouldn't live comfortably on Earth when I'm going to live comfortably for eternity. Now is not the time to retreat, but to refuse the armor of another, put on the armor of God, and stand your ground.

[11]

DAVID'S STAND

"Youth was not made for pleasure.
Youth was made for heroism."
~ Jeannie Mayo

IN THE FALL OF 2002, the doctor's reports came back with one conclusion, "Greg Puzder, you have Parkinson's Disease."

This shocking news hit our family only a few weeks after my mom's death. We sat in denial, wondering if this was truly the source of pain and shakiness that my father had been experiencing over the past few years. Our stunned faces reflected the confusion within. *How could this be true when he is only 43? This is impossible.*

Fourteen years later, we still choose to believe in faith that my dad is healed by the blood of Jesus that was shed on Calvary. Still, over the past decade, we have witnessed this once-boisterous, confident communicator and leader regress into a frail man who can barely put on his own trousers. For him, the most menial task has become as complicated as climbing Mount Everest. On more than one occasion, I have caught myself whining about the long walk across a parking lot to my car, only to remember that my father can't tie his own shoes!

This is due to the fact that Parkinson's disease causes the brain to stop producing dopamine, which results in the body not functioning properly. While the reason this occurs is unknown, researchers speculate that it is the result of being exposed to certain chemicals for a long period of time. While the cause of Parkinson's disease is not scientifically proven there are specific personality traits that correlate to this diagnosis: *uncontrollable fear* and *intense anxiety*.

My dad recalls bouts of extreme shakiness prior to school presentations or while taking a test as a college student. I don't mean shakiness associated to nervousness, but an extreme tremor that is uncontrollable. This only grew worse during the later years of his marriage to my mother. My mom's addiction and my father's controlling personality were a deadly combination as they fed each other's weaknesses.

Most of my childhood memories consist of my dad being fearful and anxious about everything from money, the future, and my mom's medical bills to small, unimportant things. It was an all-consuming anxiety that kept him awake at night and prevented true fulfillment in his life. My father missed out on so many opportunities because he just could not let go of the fear.

My dad's story is not finished. If there is one thing he would want you to learn from his journey, it's that God has not called us to sit back, be complacent, and remain silent.

When we allow fear to guide our actions rather than God's word, we will never reach our fullest potential in Christ. I firmly believe that my dad is called to preach the Gospel. Right now, this calling appears to be impossible, but I know that God is not done yet!

Let Hope Rise

"Hope. It is the only thing stronger than fear."
~ Suzanne Collins, The Hunger Games

For many years, my father succumbed to silence. Intimidation is a popular weapon of choice used by the enemy, and no person is immune. Ever since Adam and Eve were placed in the Garden of Eden, bullies have been on the prowl. In fact, one of the most epic battles in the Bible was between young David and the bully named Goliath.

Goliath, whose name literally means "giant," stood 10 feet tall and wore 126 pounds of pure armor.[9] His voice was loud and his presence dominating. For this reason, 1 Samuel 17:11 tells us, *When Saul and his troops heard the Philistine's challenge, they were terrified and lost all hope* (MSG).

One giant had the ability to strike fear and hopelessness into an entire nation. Not just any people, mind you, the people of God. This mighty nation decided to retreat in fear instead of plunging into battle. Through intimidation, Goliath had silenced every single warrior in the king's army.

However, one courageous soldier remained.

In the face of opposition, David boldly responded to the hopelessness of his nation: *"Master," said David, "don't give up hope. I'm ready to go and fight this Philistine"* (v. 32, MSG).

The nation had lost hope. When they looked at David, they saw only a weak shepherd, but God saw nothing less than a mighty warrior.

David counteracted fear with a message of hope. Jesus

Christ came to bring hope to the hopeless so that we do not have to sit silent when fear attacks. We can arise and declare the hope of Jesus Christ in the midst of our situation. Let hope rise!

Just like young David, we must carry hope into our lost and hurting world. This is not always easy. As a teenager, it was not easy to walk through my front door full of the hope of Jesus, only to be emotionally knocked down by my father. As an adult, it is not easy to minister the hope of Jesus to others while my entire family is lost in sin. It is never easy to continue to love those who persecute you, or serve those who hurt you.

The Holy Spirit dwelling within us strengthens us to praise God in the midst of suffering and darkness. We are told to rejoice in the midst of pain, because this produces hope (Romans 5:2–7). When we are filled with the light of hope, we can stare our giants in the face and say, *greater is He that is within me than he that is within the world* (1 John 4:4).

Hope has incredible power to break through the silence. It is a catalyst that will push even the weariest soldier back into battle. Hope will counteract fear every time (Job 11:18-19).

THE BATTLE LINE

> *And he [David] came to the encampment as the host was going out to the battle line, shouting the war cry. And Israel and the Philistines drew up for battle, army against army.* ~ 1 Samuel 17:20b–21, ESV

David was obviously not a swordsman or a linebacker. So, in preparation for battle, he collected five stones and stood ready to oppose his enemy.

I can imagine the little warrior taking a deep breath as he straightened his posture to its highest point. Then, from the depths of his spirit and with the loudest voice he could muster, David released a war cry that sent all fear within him fleeing. The words that flowed from this young person were strong enough to shake Heaven and Earth:

> *Then David said to the Philistine, "You come to me with a sword and with a spear and with a javelin, but I come to you in the name of the LORD of hosts, the God of the armies of Israel, whom you have defied. This day the LORD will deliver you into my hand, and I will strike you down and cut off your head. And I will give the dead bodies of the host of the Philistines this day to the birds of the air and to the wild beasts of the earth, that all the earth may know that there is a God in Israel, and that all this assembly may know that the LORD saves not with sword and spear. For the battle is the LORD's, and he will give you into our hand." When the Philistine arose and came and drew near to meet David, David ran quickly toward the battle line to meet the Philistine.*
> ~ 1 Samuel 17:45–48, ESV

David praised God as if He had already won the battle, because he viewed with spiritual eyes and knew that it had already been won. This is a powerful example of the WarCry of a king—*declaring victory in the face of impossibility*.

In his war cry, David followed a specific pattern that can help us be victorious in spiritual warfare as well:

1. First, David praised God (v. 45).

David declared that while Goliath intended to win with a sword and spear, these worldly weapons utterly failed in comparison to the name of the Lord. David proclaimed that the name of the Lord is a banner, strong tower, and refuge to all who call on Him. He alone is the God of the armies of Israel, and none can stand against Him.

Fear has a power all its own that seeks to literally paralyze or choke those who fall victim to its grip. Fear and stress even have a physical effect on our bodies. Have you ever tried to give a presentation while fearful? Your voice feels strained and forced because nerves tighten your vocal cords.

This is why David's declaration is so important! In the midst of battle, David refused to be bullied into silence. He refused to stand under the influence of fear and hopelessness, like those in his nation. His war cry announced to his enemy and all onlookers that the battle would not be won in his own strength but it belonged to the Lord.

When faced with a difficult or impossible situation, begin by praising God and declaring your enemy's weakness. Confide in some friends that can join you in declaring God's victory.

Have you or a friend been diagnosed with an illness? Praise God that, *by the stripes of Jesus Christ I am healed* (Isaiah 53:5b, KJV).

Are you believing for your family to be saved? Declare, *The promises of the Lord do not return void* (Isaiah 55:11b, KJV).

Perhaps you are struggling with fear. You can cry out, *The enemy prowls around like a roaring lion, but Jesus Christ is the Lion of the tribe of Judah, so I will not be afraid! The name of the Lord is my refuge and my strength* (1 Peter 5:8; Revelation 5:5; Psalm 46:1).

2. Second, David identifies exactly how he will defeat the enemy (v. 46).

Read through this verse again and note how specific David is when he describes the plan to defeat Goliath—even ending with the cutting off of the giant's head and feeding it to birds and beasts! It is one thing to *know* God's plan, but another thing to *declare* it in the midst of an impossible situation.

When you are faced with an impossible situation, it is powerful to identify and declare what you will do in order to gain the victory. Will you spend more time in Scripture? Will you fast? Will you forgive? Will you go out of your way to think differently? Define what you will strategically do to gain victory over your enemy.

3. Finally, David put action behind his declaration when he ran to the battle line (v.48).

This shepherd-warrior understood that one cannot declare something without also being able to stand on that declaration. As you release the WarCry of a king, be prepared to put action behind your declaration!

Notice that David did not walk or crawl to the battle line. Following the release of his war cry, David *ran quickly* toward the battle line, even while the opposing army was likely still shouting their war cry.

I can imagine this young person running boldly into his destiny while everyone else backed away. If this story were a Hollywood movie, I'm sure that the scene of David running toward the battle line would be in slow motion. Like Mel Gibson running with the American flag during *The Patriot*, there goes ruddy David, running toward the battle line!

The rest is very simple, yet often overemphasized: David slung the stone and it killed Goliath. Nothing more; nothing less. With a shepherd's staff, a bag, a few stones, and sling, David made the name of the Lord known to Israel once again by putting action behind his declaration of faith.

A WarCry is always done in love, but is not always just declared from your mouth—it is also a representation of your life. Kingdom warriors do not just declare God's victory; they live God's victory. The way in which you live for Christ determines your level of victory just as much as the words you speak. As long as you are standing for Christ everywhere you go, in both action and declaration, the Holy Spirit will penetrate your world and draw people to God.

When you speak it, you will believe it—and then, you will be able to do it!

THE WAR CRY OF A KING

David's war cry is a powerful example of what the word *rua* means. This unique Hebrew word means *to raise a shout or give a blast, such as in jubilant victory*. God spoke to my heart that this is the WarCry of a king: *to raise a declaration of God's victory in the face of impossibility*.

To be honest, I believe the battle had been won long before David sent the stone flying. The moment David released his war cry, the victory was won, because he spoke into existence that which God was confirming in his spirit (Matthew 18:18). This is due to the fact that David's victory over Goliath wasn't about David's strength with a sling; it was about David's strength in the Lord.

As you and I declare God's victory over any situation, the atmosphere of a room changes, the Earth shifts, buildings tremble, people are healed, and mere stones turn into deadly weapons. Without God Almighty, the stone was just a stone and the sling just a sling, but with God all things are possible!

Perhaps God could have used any object to kill Goliath, because the power was not in the stone but in the vessel that sent the stone flying.

An Unexpected Call

Come, let us sing for joy to the LORD; let us shout aloud to the Rock of our salvation. ~ Psalm 95:1, emphasis added

The word *shout* in this verse is the word *rua*, meaning war cry. David wrote this long after his encounter with Goliath, but I wonder if perhaps he was reminiscing on all of the wondrous victories that God had given him over the years.

Sometimes, we just have to stop and *shout* God's victory in the face of impossibility, even if it seems like the wait is long and the road is hard.

While living far away from my father, in our new rental home on the west side of Tennessee, an unexpected call came.

It was my dad.

For over a decade, I had been praying and believing that God would transform his life. On a few occasions, I even had dreams of my family sitting together and praying at the dinner table.

In reality, our dinner conversations consisted of him telling me how crazy I was for having such a radical faith. Nevertheless, this did not limit my WarCry! I continued to declare God's faithfulness in the midst of difficulty.

This call, however, came very suddenly.

The conversation began as usual, but near the end he mentioned something that nearly knocked me off my feet. My father, after living his entire life in fear and disbelief, revealed to me that he had been saved, filled with the Holy Spirit, and had received the gift of speaking in tongues. All of this happened in a matter of days, and I could tell that he was still in as much shock as I was.

After years of ridiculing me, he finally awoke from spiritual slumber. I can remember the hesitation in his voice as he mentioned the earth-shattering experiences the Lord had given him—he was saved at a church service with my aunt and then filled with the Holy Spirit after calling a Christian TV station for prayer!

Today, my father has been walking with the Lord for a few years and has officially started the journey toward inner healing. All glory to God! Even in the midst of trials, God's promises never return void. For years, I stood on the promises of God, declaring victory over a seemingly impossible giant. It all led up to this moment, an unexpected phone call that I will never forget.

Take it from my dad: Life is too short to run away from the impossible, to cower in defeat, or to allow your situation to make you a victim and fall into depression. Take smart risks, live life to the fullest, and do everything you can to fulfill your calling in Christ. Just ask my dad; a life unlived is no life at all.

Ultimately, we can charge toward the battle line with full hope in our God, or we can retreat in fear, but the latter is a life of compromise and defeat. I urge with this generation to push aside fear and realize they are warriors. Whatever fear is facing you today, decide to run head-on toward the giant and slay it, with God's words flowing through you.

Christ did not die so you can sit quietly in your comfortable home, with your ideal family, and attend a beautiful church. Rather, Christ died so we can live dangerously and do the impossible.

[12]

Mountain-Mover Generation

"With God all things are possible."
~ Matthew 19:26b

IT IS NOT UNCOMMON for me to roll into bed far past midnight on Wednesday and then sleep in on Thursday morning until the last minute possible.

However, this particular morning was different. I went to bed exhausted, but awoke abruptly at the first ray of sunlight streaming into my room.

I can recall feeling vividly wide-awake as I squinted to make out my surroundings. I thought, *"Where am I and how did I get here?"* Nothing was clear except for the oversized wall clock hanging in front of me. Its circular shape was striking against the black backdrop that surrounded me. A glow of light radiated from the clock, revealing more of its center: a black-and-white image of a snowy mountain range stood in the center of the luminous clock, undaunted by the blackness surrounding it.

At first glance, the image appeared to be a still shot, but a closer look revealed a small person, covered in snow gear, slowly trudging up the mountain toward its highest peak. Snow covered this weary traveler, but he never gave up. Nearly reaching the top, this man was equipped with his climbing gear and backpack as the clock struck midnight.

Then, I immediately woke up. Sitting straight up in bed, I felt as though I had just experienced the most restful sleep of my life. As soon as my body caught up with my mind, I turned over to grab the notebook that lay on my bedside table. I quickly drew an image of the unique clock that filled my dream only minutes before. After completing my drawing, I sat for a moment in silence listening closely for a word from the Holy Spirit.

Then I asked, "Lord, why did you show me a mountain range and weary traveler etched inside of a clock?"

The Holy Spirit responded quickly and clearly, "Because the time is now."

"The time is now for what, Lord?" I inquired.

He responded, "The time is now for the impossible. Raise up a mountain-mover generation!"

With that, the Lord put Matthew 17:20 on my heart: *"I tell you the truth, if you had faith even as small as a mustard seed, you could say to this mountain, 'Move from here to there,' and it would move. Nothing would be impossible"* (NLT).

A new word began to stir in my heart as God revealed that most of this Scripture has been heavily neglected in the church. Even I preach about having faith to move mountains, but when was that last time I actually *spoke* to the mountain in *faith?* Not with mere human words, but with a divine declaration from God.

Not only that, what does it really mean to *speak* to a mountain? What does it mean to be a mountain-mover, and what makes this generation so different?

The Lord led me to look up the original word that is translated as "mountain" in this Scripture. I discovered that the greek word is *oros*, which is not only the physical mountain that you see over the Colorado horizon, but any obstacle that may stand in one's path. In fact, "moving mountains" in Matthew 17 can be translated as *overcoming difficulty* or *accomplishing great things*.[10]

I believe Jesus could have used the word *bondage, obstacle,* or *threat* to get the point across in this Scripture, but He instead used the word *mountain*.

Why did He do this?

I think that the mental image of a mountain being picked up and thrown into the sea is something humankind views as impossible. Breaking out of chains or bondage is not an impossible feat—illusionists do it all the time. But show me someone who can move a mountain with nothing but their word; that is something to behold.

I believe Jesus used the word *mountain* because it represents the largest obstacle that has ever existed. This shows us that it is nothing compared to a little warrior who speaks a God-ordained word, even with faith as small as a mustard-seed.

Scriptures says nothing will be impossible for you, if you speak out of a heart of faith. David's mountain was a giant named Goliath. This mountain literally moved when Goliath fell to the ground after David released a declaration of faith.

Understanding that God has called you to move mountains is the key to releasing the WarCry of a king and doing the impossible in your generation.

Faith calls us to action—it calls us to be mountain-movers!

A Leap of Faith

My family loves movie night. We all cozy up next to the screen and wait expectantly for the film to begin. Even Samson, my chihuahua, gets in on the action. He often thinks of himself as Thor or Indiana Jones, and makes it his mission to ensure that everyone in the room knows it. During the fighting scenes, he will grab his little toy and violently shake his head from side to side. I think he learned this technique from watching family members get excited while watching the Miami Dolphins play.

Aside from football, my family shares a special love for the Indiana Jones series. One of our favorite scenes is when Indiana Jones finally comes to the end of his journey for the holy grail, only to discover one final obstacle: a giant chasm between the ledge he is standing on and the one he needs to get to. This is literally the last challenge before he finds the treasure on the other side.

Indy hesitantly walks up to the edge of the mountain and gazes down. Nothing but emptiness as far as the eye could see. It was too vast to jump, but there was too much at stake for him to turn back. Then, he remembers the final clue. "It's a leap of faith."

The moment of truth hit him, as he lifts his leg and takes one giant step off the edge and onto the unseen path. As he does this, the invisible pathway before him becomes visible. The path had been there all along, but a little faith was required for him to actually see it for himself.

This giant gap was the obstacle, or mountain, preventing

him from obtaining victory, but with one leap of faith the impossible became possible. Faith was the key to Indy reaching the other side of the chasm safely. He had to take a giant step of faith along the invisible path before the miracle could be birthed.

In the same way, Jesus declares that faith is the key to moving mountains. Show me a mountain-mover and I will show you someone with faith, even if their faith is as small as a mustard seed (Matthew 17:20).

However, the opposite is also true: God sees a lack of faith as a major heart issue. That is why Jesus, following his commission to move mountains, urges the disciples to walk in forgiveness and steer clear of doubt. Please understand what Jesus is saying:

> Mountain movers are not doubtful (Mark 11:22–24).
>
> Mountain movers don't harbor unforgiveness (Mark 11:25).
>
> Mountain movers speak in faith (Mark 11:23).

Unfortunately, when you allow doubt, unforgiveness, and pain to clog your heart, it will ultimately lead to a spiritual heart attack. This renders your mountain-moving power ineffective. When your heart is free, your prayers will take on a whole new power! That is why Scripture says, *The prayer of a righteous person is powerful and effective* (James 5:16b).

The power to move mountains is not in the prayer itself, but in the God-given authority of the person who prays the prayer.

When you have faith, your words become an explosive force of power in the Kingdom, which enables you to accomplish extraordinary deeds! The Lord has given you and I a combative force in prayer.

If your mountain-moving ability is lacking, it may be because you are not taking God seriously. Sometimes it is hard to believe in what you do not see, but this is exactly what you must do if you are to walk an unseen path.

Jesus told the disciples a surprising reason as to why they could not heal a girl in Matthew 17:20: *"Because you're not yet taking God seriously," said Jesus. "The simple truth is that if you had a mere kernel of faith, a poppy seed, say, you would tell this mountain, 'Move!' and it would move. There is nothing you wouldn't be able to tackle"* (MSG).

Take God seriously, because releasing a WarCry does not happen automatically. It must be strategic and consistent. Ask God to increase your faith, so that you can move mountains in the name of Jesus!

Move that Mountain

Along with Samson, my chihuahua, I also have a six-month-old red lab. His name is Chase, and his favorite pastime is to *chase* Samson around the house. Being about three times larger than him, you would think this would be a problem, but Samson is not afraid of anything.

For example, our neighbor mows his lawn with a huge riding lawn mower. As soon as the engine starts up, my two dogs immediately react.

Samson runs directly at the lawn mower and begins to bark wildly at the loud foe, as if to say, "Get away from my yard right now!"

However, if in this moment you were to look around for Chase, he would be completely missing in action. You would have to peer your head around the corner of the house in order to find him cowering behind a couch or under my legs.

Samson understands two things that Chase has yet to realize. First, Samson knows that the lawn mower cannot actually hurt him. His mommy and daddy have put a fence around the yard, so he is protected at all times. He also realizes that the lawn mower is just a loud noise. Much like the enemy who is a "roaring lion," it is all bark but no bite.

Often, God asks us to advance toward the enemy or toward the one thing that scares us. He asks us to go forward with might and power, but we are often like Chase, hiding around the corner in fear.

Know that the enemy is only *like* a roaring lion; therefore, he cannot actually harm you. God has put a hedge of protection around you and has covered you with His blood, so you can walk onto your campus or into your workplace completely protected by His Holy Spirit. You can walk straight up to a mountain, full of faith, and declare, "You must move in the name of Jesus!"

Not only *can* you do this, you *must* do this. You are commissioned to move mountains.

Part of the reason why we do not speak is that we have been taught how to worship and enjoy Christian music, but we are completely clueless when it comes to praying. This generation can praise, but it can't pray. We worship all night long, and then chant, "One more song!" We beg until the worship leaders fall over from exhaustion, but when we are asked to pray we stand by, idle and silent.

In worship, we are often participators, but when it comes to prayer, we prefer to be a spectator. Why is this?

Somewhere down the line, the enemy has distracted us,

and we have replaced praying with complaining. We claim "I don't have that spiritual gift, or that ability, or those designer clothes so what's the point in trying? My mom will never change; I will never be able to forget what he did to me; my dad will never come back. I will look dumb and I do not know what to do, so there is no point in trying!"

All the while, we fail to realize that God has not told us to speak *about* the mountain. He has called us to speak *to* the mountain!

Do you want to know the secret of reaching your world for Jesus?

Pray. Then, go out and love people. Return to your secret place and pray. Then, go out and love people again.

Leadership gurus in this generation want to give you tools, tips, and strategies for reaching people, but none of it matters if you do not know how to pray, if you don't know how to move mountains with your words. You are not called to just watch a podcast or listen to another sermon; you are called and commissioned to move mountains. Those practices will *equip* you, but only the Holy Spirit can *empower* you.

Now, it's your turn to put your faith into action. It is time to *move* that mountain, because you are a mountain-mover!

Practice speaking to the mountains in your life. Find a place to be alone and speak these promises out loud as a declaration of God's victory in the midst of impossibility:

> Because God is almighty, I declare that the local schools are free in the name of Jesus.
>
> Because God is life, I declare that the mountains of suicide and depression must be cast into the sea.

Because God is peace, I speak against the mountain of violence in my country and I declare that it will be moved in the name of Jesus.

Instead of complaining about your mountain, begin to *speak* to your mountain!

Perhaps right now your mountain is sickness, and you have been given just a few months to live. Or maybe it is an unsaved family member. Perhaps you are being bullied at work or school for being a Christian, or possibly you struggle with a financial burden. Perhaps your children are far from the Lord, or maybe you are in the midst of a major life transition. Whatever it may be, listen to the voice of the Holy Spirit; He will reveal the WarCry stirring within. Then, stand with a heart of faith and speak to the mountain!

The same faith that moves mountains also breaks chains. The same faith that moves mountains is what saved you in the first place. Christians are supposed to be the strongest people on Earth, because we have been commissioned to move mountains. Not just once or twice in our lives, but on a regular basis.

When Christians finally begin moving mountains on a regular basis, our world will begin to shake, ushering in the next move of the Holy Spirit and, eventually, the return of Christ!

The enemy seeks to silence *you* because he knows that your words have the power to silence *him*.

What are you declaring over your life? It may feel awkward at first, but I bet Jesus felt far more awkward hanging naked on the cross.

Faith may be the key to moving mountains, but speaking is the overflow of faith that actually manifests the movement!

The word *kineo* that Jesus uses in Matthew 17:20 to say that we move the mountain is the same word that refers to someone *stirring up feelings,* such as when someone says they are "moved" by a certain song.

When you speak the same words Jesus spoke, in faith, at precisely the moment He tells you to speak them, there is a release of power that can move any mountain. Imagine what is possible when you release the faith-filled WarCry that God has for you to release!

When you are preparing to move mountains, a stirring will take place deep inside your heart. Often, this stirring will continue for a long period of time, as you pray and faith is deposited, until God finally says it is time to move the mountain. It is here that faith arises and boldness overflows. At this God-ordained moment, you must cry out with a mighty WarCry and say to your mountain, "Move from here to there!"

If you don't speak to your mountain, your mountain will speak to you!

The WarCry of a king teaches you that faith is foundational to your fight; that is why it is called *the good fight of faith.* You fight with the understanding that will God empower you to win, because Jesus has already won the ultimate victory on the cross.

God revealed to me that He is stirring up an army of spiritual warriors who will usher in a release of the Holy Spirit such as the world has never known. This army will recognize that the key to moving mountains is not just having faith, but speaking in faith. This army will be a unified team of spiritual warriors, dispersed across our world for the purpose of advancing the Kingdom of God. I believe that this army will be composed of young and old, male and female, all equipped with a variety of gifts in order to carry the Holy Spirit with them wherever they go.

This is your time. This is your moment. Free of chains, ready to roar, and unafraid to take on the impossible; now is the time to uncover your authentic voice and be a mouthpiece for God in this generation.

PART 4

UNLEASH YOUR WARCRY

[13]

Army of Artists

In the beginning, God created ...
~ Genesis 1:1a

THE GOD OF THE universe and creator of all things is an artist! In fact, the very first thing we learn about God in Genesis 1:1 is that He is creative: *In the beginning, God created ...*

Our God spoke the Earth into existence, breathed life into humankind, and wove us together in our mother's womb. Scripture says He is "the Potter" and we are the "clay" (Isaiah 64:8). Nature is God's masterpiece, and humankind is His handiwork. It is undeniable that we serve a God who values creativity and innovation.

If God is an artist, and we are created in His image, then we too are artists. Christians should be the most creative, successful people on the planet, because we have access to the ultimate source of creativity and inspiration: God Himself!

Don't worry; the word *artist* refers to more than someone who paints a picture or sculpts with modeling clay. An artist is someone who is skilled at a particular task or occupation.

Every Christian should view him or herself as an artist, seeking to become skilled at the gifts the Holy Spirit has deposited in them.

Perhaps you have the ability to design (Exodus 35:3–35), or speak (Ephesians 4), or faith comes easily to you (1 Corinthians 12). The list could go on for days! I encourage you to add more gifts from Ephesians 4 and 1 Corinthians 12 to this list.

The point is that everyone has been given a measure of talent, or *spiritual gifting*. Creativity looks very different from person to person, and for good reason. My friend is a master artist when it comes to videos and graphics, but put him behind a drama script and he will struggle. Not that he is incapable of doing it, but it will not come easily to him. This does not mean that God will never ask him to act for a church production, but it does mean that he should not waste his time trying to become the next Mel Gibson.

Your calling will reflect the gift(s) that God has given you.

So, what are your gifts?

Discover Your Gifts

As servants in the body of Christ, we should meet each need we see. (*see a need, meet a need.*) It is unbiblical to *only* do that which we are good at. For example, the person who declares, "I cannot clean the bathroom, because I am not gifted with a toilet brush" is quite deceived.

However, you will only find true satisfaction in life by skillfully using your God-given gifts to build up the body of Christ.

To help you discover your top spiritual gifts, I recommend that you take a spiritual gifts assessment.

Recognizing and awakening your gifts are key to

unleashing your WarCry. However, the enemy knows this truth as well, and he will do everything he can to stop you from functioning in your gifts.

Stir Up Your Gifts

Stirring up your gifts is much more difficult than identifying them, because fear will always counteract your gifts. This is one of the enemy's main strategies to keep you silent.

For many years, I lived under the bondage of fear. Unable to stand on the promises of God. I was not using the gifts God had given me, and I was depressed by the fact that fear prevented me from even trying.

After years of running from my calling, I decided that I was more afraid of not following the will of God than I was of being afraid. The enemy had attacked my throat by bringing about hypothyroidism, but God completely healed me. The enemy has tried to silence me through fear, but He who is within me is stronger than he who is within the world (1 John 4:4). I decided that I would not respond to the lies of this world in the same way that my family had; I would rise up and walk in my destiny instead.

Do you know what broke the intimidation off my life?

It broke when I began functioning in the gifts that I knew God had given me, even in the midst of being anxious and afraid.

The enemy will try to prevent you from using your gifts by telling you that you should wait until you are older, more qualified, or better trained. However, Scripture states that the only way to break off fear and intimidation is to do that which you are called to do!

Essentially, you must *do it afraid*. Listen to the Apostle Paul:

*Therefore I remind you that you **stir up the gift of God,** which is in you by the laying on of my hands.* ***For God has not given us the spirit of fear,*** *but of power, and love, and self-control.* ~ 2 Timothy 1:6–7, MEV, emphasis added

Scripture tells us to stir up the gift of God.
Why is this so essential?
Because God has not given us a spirit of fear!

Pastor Timothy needed to hear this message, because he had been silenced by the intimidation of those around him. As a result, his gifts became inactive and his war cry was silenced. In this Scripture, Paul is urging Timothy to stir up his gift (or, begin functioning in his gifts again) with boldness, rather than allowing other people to intimidate him.

The enemy sends a spirit of fear to counteract the Holy Spirit. A spirit of fear is always sent to prevent you from being fully empowered for the work at hand, to stop you in your tracks, and to paralyze you. But remember, God has not given you a spirit of fear!

So, how do you stir up your gift?

The answer is simple, but so very difficult. You must begin using your gifts (or begin using them again). Fear and complacency will try to prevent you from stirring up your gifts, but the only way to break the intimidation is to use your gifts!

Never Stop Using Your Gifts

Warriors are *not* born; they are made. After you discover and begin stirring up your gifts, you must put them into action on a regular basis.

Practice, prepare, study, and do whatever you have to do to become more skilled, but don't let the gift lay dormant inside of you. Don't be scared of your gift, and do not be afraid that you don't measure up to someone else with the same gift. Remember the parable of the talents in Matthew 15:14–30? The servant who buried his gift ended up losing it. Do not bury your gift. Utilize it with full confidence that God is on your side.

Don't wait another moment. Release your song. Release your cry. Release your paintbrush. Release your instrument. Release your dance. Release your words. As you release the gift that God has put inside of you, the anointing will flow, lives will be transformed, the Body of Christ will be built up, and people will come to know Jesus.

Even now, I believe God is preparing His generals and placing them in strategic positions all over the world. They will be unlikely leaders who will rise up out of the ashes. They may not be mighty in stature, but God's anointing will be all over their gifts.

I urge you to discover your gifts, stir them up, and never stop using them.

An Unforeseen Force

One summer night, I was sitting in the lower left corner of the Ohio Conference Center in the among of 10,000 students from across the nation. This was the final service of the National Fine Arts Festival.

The service went as usual, but as the evening drew to a close something unforeseen took place. Frightening news was delivered from the stage that a terrorist organization had just launched a social media attack on the United States. The target was young people, and the goal was to overwhelm social media with derogatory messages in order to enlist American youth to join radical Islam.

Not only was this the first terrorist recruitment plot ever launched on social media, it was one of the few times in history that young people were the target of such a mass movement for evil. A similar attempt took place many years ago, when a man named Hitler sought to recruit young people for his army of mass destruction. This time, however, social media was at the heart of the attack.

The moment that this information was released, the packed conference center fell into complete silence as everyone eagerly awaited further information. We were all wondering, *Had they succeeded? How many young people were seduced by the messages? How many had been recruited? How would this affect us?*

To grasp the magnitude of this situation, you have to understand the impact that social media has on culture. One comment about a public figure, whether positive or negative, can swarm across the world in a matter of moments, and millions of people have access to it in a split second.

Had the enemy succeeded in this social media attempt, who knows the number of young people who would have enlisted in this army? While many were affected and did respond to join this movement, many more were distracted by comments surrounding another event.

Our event.

At that moment, only a few events were trending higher on social media than the terrorist group. One of them was our event, #Columbus14.

Every time a person hashtagged our event, it directed attention away from the terrorist group and toward a God-centered gathering.

This is the power of a WarCry.

For one of the first times in history, an army of believers raised a WarCry through technology. Our group was able to overwhelm social media with one voice. Little did this terrorist group know that, the very same day they had planned their attack, God had also prepared an army of young people with a mission to lift up the name of Jesus. A weapon did form against us, but it did not prevail!

This encounter left me shaken to the core. Right in the midst of writing this book, God allowed me to witness firsthand one of the most powerful examples of a WarCry that this nation has ever seen.

Our social media cry not only rocked the U.S., but shook every other nation as well, because the terrorist realized that American youth were not as disconnected from reality as they had thought. We do have something to stand for, and His name is Jesus. Our God is not dead; He is alive and is releasing a roar in this generation through surrendered disciples.

However, I would venture to say that the majority of youth in the arena that night failed to recognize the magnitude of what had just taken place. Had this effort to enlist American students for a terrorist army gone unchecked, who knows the amount of youth that may have been persuaded to join this deadly terrorist group!

God had clearly raised up an army of passionate believers to drown out the voice of the enemy. That sound was the cry of 10,000 students giving glory to God. This corporate WarCry of an entire group of people was so loud that it silenced a recruitment plot that was sent to the heart of America—directly at her young people.

There is no doubt in my mind that this is the most creative and innovative generation that has ever walked the planet.

Together, we are an unforeseen force.

The enemy knows that if he can silence one instrument, the orchestra will not resound. We are the instruments that the Lord plays for His glory. If one instrument is silent, the orchestra will be lacking. Whether our instrument is in the area of artistry, music, preaching, serving, or supporting, we all play a vital note in the body of Christ.

The wars and rumors of wars in our society are not a physical problem, but a spiritual problem. The spiritual realm is shaking, and the Earth is feeling her labor pains. I believe that God is preparing to move through new areas of technology, and unlikely people of all ages. It is only a matter of time before there are disciples in every area of society that will shine the light of God's presence into dark places.

Imagine a world where every member of the body of Christ stands unafraid and unashamed for Jesus, utilizing their gifts for the glory of God in our broken world. Every area of society would be affected, and no one would be jealous of another, because they would be captivated by what God is doing. Our WarCry would be so loud that it would overtake social media and shake the world.

There is a strong conviction in my heart that God is raising up such an army, one that knows the power of God's word inside of them and is not afraid to unleash their WarCry. This is a unique army that has never walked the face of the Earth before—an army of artists.

Let's take a look at *your* role in this army.

[14]

UNLEASHED

"I am not afraid. I was born to do this."
~ Joan of Arc

WHAT DOES IT MEAN to live a life that is completely *unleashed?*

I am confident that my 80-pound lab, Chase, knows the answer to this question better than anyone else.

When Chase is on his leash, he is at the mercy of the person walking him. When he was a puppy, this was no easy task, as Chase resisted the leash as often as possible, running left and right in an effort to break free. He even attempted to chew through the leash itself, and sometimes succeeded.

Every time Chase is constrained by the leash, I am sure he is dreaming about his next moment of freedom.

Then, the moment finally arrives. His little heart begins to beat fast and his green eyes dart back and forth as the leash is carefully removed from his collar. At this point, Chase does not casually stroll away with a smile on his face. On the contrary, he forcefully launches himself toward freedom.

As believers, we often find ourselves held back by a leash.

The question is, who holds the other end?

Satan often tries to choke us into silence with a leash of lies, because he does not want us to live in full confidence of the power of our voice. He knows if our voice is unleashed, we will be a force to be reckoned with.

At times, God will hold our voice back, because it is not yet time for us to go forth in power. As Scripture explains, there is a time to speak and a time to be silent (Ecclesiastes 3:7). If we obey God in the silent season, He will strengthen us to speak words of life and power in the right season.

However, more often than not, you actually hold the other end of your own leash and are held back by nothing other than your own lack of understanding of your true identity.

Who am I? What was I born to do? How can I make a difference? Confusion clogs the heart and overwhelms the mind, permanently trapping you beneath a sea of uncertainty.

On the contrary, a life unleashed is one of clarity and discernment; it is a life of confidence in your voice as an individual and how you can use your voice to impact your generation.

Your voice is *An instrument or medium of expression; the right of expression; influential power.*[11]

A WarCry is not always expressed by your words, but it is always declared with your voice.

By "voice," I mean both the words that flow from your mouth and all aspects of your identity, because your voice is much louder than your words.

Your voice is the instrument or tool by which you express yourself. It is a combination of your gifts, purpose, and personality. It is an expression of your passion that erupts to impact those around you.

God gives each of us a voice, and, as we surrender to Him, He slowly reveals to us more about who we are and how our voice can make a difference in this world.

Some voices are assertive and challenging, while others are more gentle and nurturing. God has created certain voices to be more logical and others to be more creative. There is beauty in diversity!

We are not limited by our weaknesses; rather, we all work together to glorify God. In order to add lasting value to this world, we must each find our voice.

To help you break through uncertainty, I will address specific questions that will help you uncover your God-given voice. In this world of confusion and chaos, this will empower you to *live unleashed*.

Unleash Your Voice

Finding and unleashing your voice does not typically happen by accident. It is a lifelong process of surrendering to God and growing through experiences that shape your voice.

Why not begin this journey today?

Discover your values

Your values are foundational core beliefs that inform your opinions, decisions, and actions. They are *your* judgment of what is important in *your* life (not what your parents, teachers, leaders, or friends think is best for you).

Identifying your values will help you understand more about who you are and why you do certain things.

Here are some of my core values in the area of family:

- Aside from my relationship with God, my family is the

most important thing to me.

- I believe that my husband and I should both equally serve and prayerfully make decisions together for our family.

It's your turn! Off the top of your head, write down one or two things you value in the areas of spirituality, family, and work. Your answers will be a guide to help you understand your internal make-up.

Now, ask yourself, "Am I being true to *my* values, or am I pretending to share the values of other people so that I fit in?" If you compromise your values in order to hang out with certain people, even if they are Christians, you are in a place of compromise. This is because your values will not allow you to comfortably act in a way that is not in line with who you truly are!

This may explain why you have a difficult time being bold in certain contexts, or working with certain people; because their values do not reflect yours, causing you to become silent. Knowing these predispositions will help you be more aware of your response in certain situations.

WHAT IS YOUR WHY?

Your *why* is the greatest thing that captivates your heart. It is something that causes your emotions to rise up and urges you to respond.

If you have a big enough *why*, then everything else will follow. If you don't have a big enough *why*, then you will be discouraged and unfulfilled by the work that you do.

You can understand more about your *why* by looking at what makes you passionate. Passion leads you to impact the lives of others and is a burning fire inside of your heart that will keep you moving forward.

Every person is passionate about something. I am talking about the unrelenting urge that leads you to step out in faith, regardless of what seems realistic. For example, I am passionate about empowering others, promoting equality between men and women, diversity, and preaching God's word.

Of the top of your head, write down three things that evoke the greatest passion in your life.

Now, let's move on to a more practical question.

WHAT NEED CAN YOU MEET?

If you feel purposeless or lost in life, you may not have realized what problem God put you on this Earth to solve. The beginning of your *why* stems from the understanding that God has called every believer to be a solution to the greatest problem on this Earth: *There are lost and hurting people who need to hear about Jesus.* We must pray, go, give, and speak so that people can hear.

However, there are also needs that only you can meet, due to your unique make-up. Perhaps you are called to be an answer to the sickness in this world by becoming a doctor. Maybe you are called to be a mother to a child who would otherwise be alone. Are you called to start a ministry that reaches those who are suffering? Could there be a church in need of a strong youth pastor with your type of vision?

Based on your answers so far, name one overwhelming need that you think God has put you here to solve. This need may be something you can do now, or it may be something that God will have you do in the future.

Prayerfully consider these things, and do not be discouraged if you cannot answer these questions right now.

Authentic and Unleashed

People often talk about "calling" as if there is only one significant thing you will ever do with your entire life. I believe that life is full of a series of callings, one after another. In each calling, you learn more about your voice and how you can bring meaning into this world.

At the beginning of my journey, it was hard to avoid merely following the trends. I was confused about my values, which seemed to contradict those of many other church leaders. I was confused about my passions, because they were unusual for someone from my background.

What I realized is the journey to understanding who I am is a process, and each experience reveals another layer of discovering my passion, purpose, and potential. Who I am today is the result of following the soft utterance of the Holy Spirit into moments and opportunities that bring God glory.

For example, God called me to do creative arts in one season of my life, but the passion revealed to me in that season is central to who I am now; it is part of my authentic voice. I could not see it then, but this calling revealed to me more about my voice as a minister, because it taught me the importance of empowering everyone, regardless of age or skill type.

Ultimately, it requires bravery to become all that God has called you to be.

God gives you permission to be you and the ability to embrace the values that make up who you are, to run after the passion that gives you meaning in life, to confront what gives you doubt and respond, *I will not be afraid. This is what I was born to do.*

Romans 12:2 (MSG) explains this further:

> *Embracing what God does for you is the best thing you can do for him. Don't become so well-adjusted to your culture that you fit into it without even thinking. Instead, fix your attention on God. You'll be changed from the inside out. Readily recognize what he wants from you, and quickly respond to it. Unlike the culture around you, always dragging you down to its level of immaturity, God brings the best out of you, develops well-formed maturity in you.*

Kingdom warriors do not fit in with culture; they change culture.

Embracing Jesus and accepting who God has made you to be is the best thing that you can do for the Kingdom. The trends and fads of this world will fade, but the Word of God will live forever!

It gives me peace to know that God is making me into who I'm called to be. I feel a load lifted from my shoulders when I remember that it is not up to me to create who I am, only to actively engage in discovering who I am.

By listening to the voice of the Holy Spirit and learning to navigate through the seasons of life, you too will continue to learn more about your unique voice. There is creativity, passion, and vision already inside of you, because the Holy Spirit dwells within your heart. Stop striving for perfection and begin simply abiding in God's presence, trusting that He will make you who He created you to be.

> *Your voice reflects a clear understanding of who you are and infuses it with the best of who you are.*[12]

I encourage you to spend some time reflecting on your voice. It may be obvious to you, or God may be slowly revealing it to you. Before you ask for advice from other people in this process, first ask the Holy Spirit for advice. You can also go back and look at the answers to your questions in order to see if you can recognize any patterns. These patterns reveal a common passion and purpose that God has placed deep within your heart, which is your *authentic voice*.

I pray that you have gained more clarity in grasping your authentic voice, but it is not enough to just answer a few questions. You must *accept* the mission and *choose* to live dangerously.

[15]

LIVE DANGEROUSLY

*"When written in Chinese, the word 'crisis' is composed
of two characters. One represents danger
and the other represents opportunity."*
~ President John F. Kennedy

GOD IS GOOD, BUT He is also a warrior. He is loving and compassionate, but He is also wild and dangerous. He calls you and me to live dangerously, to do things that often don't make sense, and to trust Him in the midst of it.

Often, the bigger the mountain, the harder it is to trust God. However, these are the moments when we must trust Him the most. On the other side of the mountain is a new level of victory, if we determine in our hearts to never give up.

I recently had an encounter with a large mountain. Surrounded by nothing but desert, dirt, and hot sun, my husband and I began to question whether or not the hike to the Hollywood sign was really worth it.

I glanced over at Joe, who looked as if he was going to pass out any minute. One of his footsteps was about four of mine, so I was confident that I looked just as exhausted. Needless to say, this was way out of our normal exercise routine. Not to mention that the flat landscape of Florida was nothing compared to the mountainous trails of California!

After putting one foot in front of the other for forty-five minutes, we finally rounded the final turn and climbed the last few steps. Our reward was a bird's-eye view of the entire city of Los Angeles, and beyond. It stands as one of the most breathtaking moments in my life, or maybe that was the lack of oxygen from the climb. Either way, the renowned Hollywood sign stood, directly below us, shining flawlessly in the California sun.

In that moment, I realized why athletes prepare for years prior to scaling Mount Everest or attempting an Ironman triathlon. One wrong move, and you die. You have to study the terrain, physical limitations, and environmental adjustments.

The more dangerous the task, the more preparation is required.

Even though it crossed our minds that quitting might have been the best option, I am so glad we pushed through. More importantly, I am grateful that, despite being on vacation, we did not pick the comfort of our couch over the intensity of a hike. Instead, we decided to live dangerously.

Passion is *a strong feeling that causes you to act in a dangerous way*.[13] Passion compels us to do things we would not normally do. It pushes us beyond our limitations and begs that we do not give up.

I believe it is the same in our walk with the Lord. God has not called us to live comfortably, but to live dangerously. In fact, handling the word of God is dangerous, because it is a sword that we must learn to wield properly. Praying is dangerous work, because it is marked by spiritual warfare.

Releasing a WarCry is dangerous, because it involves taking a stand against opposition.

Listen closely: God did not save you to keep you silent. He died to make you dangerous.

Armed and Dangerous

Have you, or someone you know, ever been the victim of harsh rumors? Know that you are not alone! Jesus, the coolest dude in all of history, was also the recipient of false rumors. That is exactly why He asked those closest to him one of the most profound questions in all of Scripture.

> *When Jesus came to the region of Caesarea Philippi, he asked his disciples, "Who do people say the Son of Man is?" They replied, "Some say John the Baptist; others say Elijah; and still others, Jeremiah or one of the prophets." "But what about you?" he asked. "Who do you say I am?"* ~ Matthew 16:13–15

I believe this is not just a question for the original twelve disciples; it is also a question for our generation. People are spreading rumors about Jesus in our generation:

Atheists say He's a myth.
Muslims say He's just another good prophet.
Buddhists say He's not the only way to the Father.
I bet many of your peers would say Jesus is a waste of time.

All the while, Jesus is pressing in and whispering, *Who do you say I am? In a world of deception, can you clearly see My identity?*

In verse 16, Simon Peter is the first to answer. Spend a moment meditating on his bold response:

> *"You are the Messiah, Son of the living God." Jesus replied, "Blessed are you, Simon son of Jonah, for this was not revealed to you by flesh and blood, but by my Father in heaven. And I tell you that you are Peter,*

and on this rock I will build my church, and the gates of Hades will not overcome it." ~ Matthew 16:16–18

I can imagine a smile spreading across the face of Jesus as Peter publicly recognizes Him as the Messiah. As a result, Jesus will now identify this bold disciple by a new name. He will no longer be Simon (small stone), but Peter (large rock). Not only that, but on Peter's solid confession of who He is, Jesus will build the Church!

Peter's declaration revealed the content of his heart.

When Jesus responded, "I will build My Church," He wasn't referring to a beautiful building or a good-looking group of people. *Ekklesia,* the original used for *Church,* referred to a branch of the Greek government that was responsible for military strategy and declaring war. The Church is the spiritual military base on Earth, an army of people that advance God's Kingdom.

The Church was made for battle. Not only are we called to live dangerously, but we are also called to be dangerous to the kingdom of darkness. Jesus says that His church will be so expansive with energy, so dangerous, that not even the gates of Hell will be able to hold it back.

Your WarCry is one way that God makes you dangerous, because it is an overflow of the Holy Spirit from within you and enters this world like dynamite! The enemy is scared of your voice. That is why he wants to silence you, so that you cannot speak. However, God is calling you speak.

Speak to the giants (1 Samuel 17:45–47).
Speak to the mountains (Mark 11:20–25).
Speak to impossible situations (Mark 4:39).
Speak freedom to your household (John 8:36).

Speak against the chains in your country (Psalm 107:14).
Speak to your generation, that it will see revival (Psalm 67:4–5).
Speak to the nations, that they will see breakthrough (Psalm 33:12).

Not only am I saying you shouldn't be silent; I am conveying that it has been the enemy's tactic since the beginning of time to silence you. He wants to make you complacent, distracted, lustful, afraid, doubtful, and lazy, because he is afraid of you!

Sarah, a homeschooled student in Florida, decided she would not allow complacency and distraction to hold her back. One would think that the label of "homeschooler" would have hindered Sarah's ability to reach her world. Knowing Sarah personally, I can honestly say this label only made her more determined to be dangerous to the kingdom of darkness.

After years of leading worship at her parents' church, Sarah decided that the best place for her to be a warrior for Christ was at the local high school campus in her city. So, she began to attend the after-school campus club, even though she did not attend the school.

Soon after, God birthed a dream in Sarah's heart so big that it seemed impossible, especially for a homeschooler. The chains at her school were strong and the walls were high, but God called Sarah to be victorious.

This mighty leader organized a huge outreach on the football field one Friday night. The club invited the entire school to a time of prayer, worship, and creative arts.

This may not sound like something that high school students would be interested in, but over 200 people showed up. Sarah led worship, some student performed a "human video," and they closed in prayer by encircling the entire football field.

Sarah's own words give a description of her WarCry that night:

> This is what a faith-filled school looks like. 240 students praying and singing "Amazing Grace" tonight on the football field at Bell High School. God isn't finished. He's got His hand on this generation!

Sarah's WarCry, which consisted of her gifts, passion, and purpose, was unleashed in a unique way that night. This was a student who decided to live dangerously and inspired many others to do the same. She pushed past labels and fear, so that she could make a difference in her community.

In the same way, the world labeled Peter as a reckless screw-up, but God looked past that label and said, "You are Peter, and you are called to be dangerous to the kingdom of darkness." People will label you unwanted, unimportant, uncool, but when you know the Lord, then He looks past the labels that others give you and tells you who you really are.

With this new identity comes the authority to walk in power. Jesus does not give His power to just anyone; He gives His power to those whom He trusts.

Just like Sarah and Peter, you will only effectively unleash a WarCry if you understand that you are armed with the Holy Spirit and called to be dangerous to the kingdom of darkness.

I love Paul's perspective on this:

> **And why do you think I keep risking my neck in this dangerous work?** I look death in the face practically every day I live. Do you think I'd do this if I wasn't convinced of your resurrection and mine as guaranteed by the resurrected Messiah Jesus?
> ~ 1 Corinthians 15:30–31, MSG, emphasis added

Being dangerous does not mean being reckless, it means being unashamedly righteous. That is exactly why living dangerously is less about your strength and more about your surrender. There is safety in remaining silent, but God is not calling you to safety.

We serve a creative, radical, wild God! Let's be inspired by His example to live dangerously and make the most of every opportunity.

Our Mockingjay

Katniss Everdeen understood what it meant to live dangerously. She lived in the most desolate area of a corrupt nation, led by a dictator who felt he had to execute young people in order to maintain power. This execution was packaged in a brutal game in which children fought to the death. Most of you know this movie. It is, of course, *The Hunger Games*. I believe that this movie connects with our generation so strongly because we love to see the underdog overcome all odds and rise as the hero.

Without any desire to fight, Katniss was thrust to the battle line and forced into war. The cry of Katniss was birthed from a desire to save her sister, but it turned into a WarCry that motivated the entire nation. Her voice brought together all twelve districts and eventually made her the face of the revolution as she became their Mockingjay.

In the same way, I wonder what the WarCry of our generation is? What do we get excited about? What do we long for? What are we willing to fight for? I think a few of the things we for are: opportunity, equality, individuality, and creativity.

Our generation is unprecedented. We break new ground and seek to make our mark on the world. We are so hungry to make a difference and change our culture, but it seems like everywhere we turn there are obstacles, anxiety, confusion, unrest, and louder voices that try to silence us.

Like the corrupt nation in *The Hunger Games*, our generation thinks we need a mockingjay, someone to lead us into victory. So we cry out:

> *If someone would mentor me, I would have a better life.*
>
> *If we only had a different president, our problems in our world would go away.*
>
> *If only a new Christian leader would write a book that would catch my attention and entertain me, my life would be different.*

We cry out for someone to stand up and be our mockingjay, a leader worth following. The truth is that we do not need to search for a mockingjay, because Jesus is the mockingjay. He already came, died, and rose again so we could be free. He is the leader worth following.

I propose that what we need is for Christians rise up and say, "I will not be silent." Let our generation be characterized by the *right* kind of outcry—one that reflects the voice of Jesus.

What would it look like if our generation released a WarCry that honored Jesus? I am not exactly sure, but I know that it is going to happen. I know that God is putting people in place right now to speak out on His behalf. I urge you to join God's army. Learn to unleash your voice, so that you can help craft the WarCry of your generation.

Today, at this very moment, you have a reason to rise up. You have the ability to unleash your voice. You have what it takes to impact your world.

When you understand your voice and use it to further the Kingdom of God, you will be more alive, awake, and on fire to reach your world. When other people can sense your WarCry through the words you speak and the life you live, they will be inspired to live on fire for Jesus as well.

We need you. Do not abandon the mission. You are not a disappointment, and your contribution will not go to waste. If you quit, you will spend your life wishing you had a purpose.

Understand that you were created to be you. Your personality, gifting, and DNA were not an accident. One of the greatest traps that a Christian can fall victim to is the notion that they need to "change" who they are in order to accomplish the will of God in their lives. While we do need to change negative habits and destructive behavior, we do not need to change our personalities. Instead, we are called to discover the power that dwells within the unique make-up of each and every one of us, and unleash it for the entire world to see.

WarCry, Unleashed

A WarCry has the ability to unite all believers under the common cause of *knowing Jesus and making His name known in all the Earth.*

Our voices do not all sound the same, but we share the same *motivation* to see the name of Jesus spread to every corner of the Earth. This is carried out in different ways, by different people. However, we all share the same *love* (Matthew 22:37–39).

When grounded in God's love, your unique voice will give rise to your WarCry, which is your voice unleashed. It is as unique as you are, and will always be an expression of the things that are most important to you in each season and to serve a particular purpose. By walking in your calling, you will express your WarCry by the way you live and the words you speak. To know your WarCry is to be unashamed of who you are in Christ and able to express it through your authentic voice.

The three Hebrew words for war cry are:

Teruah – Sound the alarm for battle.

Tsarach – Release a roar that breaks chains.

Rua – Declare God's victory in the face of impossibility.

A WarCry can take many forms. Sometimes, your primary cry is a desire for intimacy with the Lord. Other times, your WarCry will be a tool used to break chains. At some point, you will be faced with a mountain, and a cry for God to do the impossible will be released.

Remember, our God is a creative God who has given each of us a *voice*. Our job is to find our voice, and use it to speak to our world. **Your WarCry is your personal voice set on fire by God's power.** It is no longer just you, but God speaking *through* you. That is why you are able to break chains and move mountains, because your voice takes on God's power.

What does *your* WarCry sound like?

It will be as unique as you, and will be revealed to you by God—the One who gave you a voice in the first place.

If you look at the most influential people throughout history, they each understood their unique voice. They knew that their personal expression would be timeless in a world of posers and ever-changing fads. They knew their authentic voice would transcend culture, because fads did not determine their work. They were brave enough to sift through misleading influences to discover their true voice and actually change culture, instead of just fitting in. They understood that the goal of developing an authentic voice was not to benefit themselves, but to awaken others to things they never thought they could accomplish.

When your voice is unleashed, it becomes a WarCry, a mighty wake-up call to your generation.

Never become so fearful that you choose to give instead of trusting God and moving forward.

It is time to dream again. It is time to fight again. Allow God to stir your heart and take you to a deeper level of faith. Then, open your mouth and speak!

God, I surrender fully to You. I ask You to continue revealing to me the authentic voice that You have put inside of me. Show me the gifts and passions that make me who I am. Then, unleash my voice as a mighty WarCry, so that I can break the silence off of my generation. Amen.

A Challenge to the "Now" Generation

MY HEART BREAKS FOR this generation, which has not-so-lovingly been dubbed the *"now" generation*. Many believe that the "now" generation is sick with *instant gratification syndrome*. Namely, they want fancy cars, huge houses, and successful careers—**now**.

This title has been given to those who between the ages of thirteen and to forty. Rather than taking the unseen path, which is often filled with obstacles and only navigated by the GPS of faith, many believe this generation seeks to avoid the hard road at all costs. Right now, America is in a desert season, but God is saying, "Forget the past, I am doing a new thing! I will put an unseen path in the middle of your wilderness and rivers in your dry place!" (Isaiah 43:19, paraphrased).

I feel like Elijah, praying for rain to fall on this generation, or like David, declaring God's victory in the face of impossibility. My heart burns to see young men and woman push aside the comforts of this world and begin to walk the unseen path.

In fact, I declare we are the "now" generation—not because we want blessings now, but because the time for world-shaking revival is now! When I look through spiritual eyes, I do not see a selfish generation; I see an army that honors innovation and creativity.

Do not give up on this generation! Do not give up on each

other! I have seen God at work among these young adults. It is time for the "now" generation to arise. When God speaks a word, nothing can stand against it. Not the pain of your past or previous failures, or current insecurities. My personal story screams this just as loud as any.

I'm sure you have seen at least one of those links on Facebook that urge you to take a test created by an "expert" in order to help you become a better leader. I recently came across such a list. This assessment consisted of various childhood scenarios that were most likely to cause someone to be insecure. Since insecurity is a root to many detrimental flaws, I decided this was a list that needed some attention.

What I discovered was quite discouraging. I found myself checking every box on the list of circumstances most likely to cause someone to be insecure.

Raised in a broken home ... check.
Addicted parent ... check.
Traumatic death of a parent as a child ... check.

The list went on and on. I kid you not, I was qualified to check every box on the list.

According to the world, I have no right to tell you not to be silent. According to the world, I should be attending therapy every week. But, according to the standard to which I measure my life, I declare that Jesus Christ has restored me, and now I live my life with a shout that He is Lord. I declare that I am healed and I am set free from every generational bondage orchestrated by the enemy.

Don't let another day go by where you find yourself chained to the snare of silence. Your story is not over. It is a legend in the making that has only just begun.

I challenge you to walk the unseen path, that God sets before you to dream bigger than anyone in your family has ever dreamed before, to cry out for an awakening in your generation. I dare you to unleash your WarCry. If you do not stand for something, you will fall for anything. Jesus is the only eternal prize worth standing for. Mark my words: if you do not unashamedly stand for God, you will cower to the standards of man. **But you, warrior, were not created to fit in with your culture. You were created to be set apart, unique, distinct, and dangerous.**

This is the rally cry I speak over my generation:

- I see a generation that fearlessly walks unseen paths by faith, rather than stumbling along the road of instant gratification.

- I see a generation of men and women fighting together to see the Kingdom of God revealed.

- I see a generation of leaders who work hard and pray even harder.

- I see a generation that functions in the supernatural on a regular basis, not just on rare occasions.

- I see a generation that sees worship as a transformational way of life, rather than a religious activity to be fulfilled.

- I see a generation full of creativity and innovation.

- I see a generation of warriors who know that their weakness is not a setback, but a set-up to be used by

God.

I pray that you have heard the wake-up call and are inspired to raise a WarCry in your world. Hear me loud and clear, none of this is possible without the Holy Spirit.

"What ever happened to Pentecost?"

This question plagues my mind and overwhelms my soul. Where is the urgency and the hunger that once marked our generation? Where is the relentless urge to share the Gospel that marked the disciples and created the early Church? Where is the fulfillment of Jesus' promise: *Very truly I tell you, whoever believes in me will do the works I have been doing, and they will do even greater things than these, because I am going to the Father* (John 14:12)?

I urge my generation to return to the source of power that once characterized the early Church in a great way. You cannot reach your world without God's anointing, without the Holy Spirit.

It is not by force nor by strength, but by my Spirit, says the LORD of Heaven's Armies. ~ Zechariah 4:6, NLV

Do not treat Pentecost as though it is a story from a novel. Treat it as though it is your life-blood, the source of all that you do for the Kingdom.

Where did Pentecost go? It has been dwelling silently in the heart of every believer.

They can forbid teachers to pray at school. They can remove the name of Jesus from your workplace. They can even take the phrase, "One nation under God," out of the pledge of allegiance, but they cannot take the Holy Spirit out of *you*.

Everywhere you go, Jesus goes. Since the world cannot

take Jesus out of you, it will try to silence you. Therefore, I encourage you:

For all who are ready to take a stand against the silence of our generation, know that once God has revealed to you an area of brokenness, it is your responsibility to do something about it.

For those of you who are still waiting for your mission: if there is still breath in your lungs, you are here for a purpose. God is not finished with you yet. If you are sick of the silence and ready for an awakening, here is your challenge:

Continue to develop your authentic voice.

It is a journey.

Be fearless as you unleash your WarCry.

It is a necessity.

Relentlessly break through the silence of your generation.

It is your responsibility.

With the knowledge and empowerment that you have gained, go and shake this world with your unique voice as expressed through a mighty WarCry!

One night the Master spoke to Paul in a dream: "Keep it up, and don't let anyone intimidate or silence you."
~ Acts 18:8–11, MSG

NOTES

1) *Ten Year Old Girl Saves Dozens From Tsunami*. The Sun - UK. January, 2005. http://www.rense.com/general61/tele.htm.
2) Ibid.
3) Ibid.
4) Ibid.
5) *MTV is Rock Around the Clock*. Philadelphia Inquirer, Nov. 3, 1982.
6) *Telemachus - January 1, 404 AD the END of Gladiator Games in Rome*. September, 2009. http://www.theroadtoemmaus.org/RdLb/31JdXn/Christnty/SpWr/Telemachus.html
7) *WWII Prisoner of War Converted, Becomes Missionary to Japan*. Christianity Today International, 1997. http://www.preachingtoday.com/illustrations/2009/may/7051809.html
8) *Knight's Armor*. March 13, 2015. http://www.lordsandladies.org/knights-armor.htm
9) Strong's Concordance via Biblehub.com
10) Ibid.
11) Merriam-Webster Dictionary (online edition).
12) Todd Henry, *Louder Than Words* (New York: Penguin Random House LLC, 2015), 10.
13) Merriam-Webster Dictionary. (online edition).

Acknowledgements

Thank you to my husband, Joe. You are my closest friend and forever confidant. God knew that your encouragement would sustain me on this journey. You are truly one of a kind.

I'm thankful to my father, Greg Puzder, for allowing me to write about his experiences in life. Thank you for never giving up, even during the hardest of times.

Thanks to Jared Stump, Joy Henley, and Battle Ground Creative publishing for your guidance and hard work on this project. This would not have happened without you!

And the biggest thank you of all I give to my Lord and Savior, Jesus Christ.

About the Author

Natalie Barnoske is an anointed speaker and ordained minister with the Assemblies of God, who is passionate about seeing this generation encounter Pentecost. She and her husband, Joe, are the founders of Pen Florida Youth Alive, a missions organization that empowers students to impact their schools. Natalie and Joe live in Lakeland, Florida, with their two dogs, Samson and Chase. To learn more, please visit www.nataliebarnoske.com.

Proudly Supported by Pen Florida Youth Alive

Equipping and empowering the next generation to reach the lost and the hurting in their schools.

www.pfyouthalive.com

Other resources by Natalie Barnoske:

EmpowerME Challenge

The Movement Series

www.ingramcontent.com/pod-product-compliance
Lightning Source LLC
Chambersburg PA
CBHW070150100426
42743CB00013B/2863